University

The
Students, Faculty,
and Campus Life at One
University

University

Alvin Schwartz

*The
Students,
Faculty,
and Campus Life at
One University,
profusely illustrated
with photographs*

The Viking Press   **New York**

The introductory comment by Arthur Miller is from
"University of Michigan," an article which appeared in
the December 1953 issue of *Holiday* Magazine

Contents

It was . . . the testing ground for all my prejudices, my beliefs, and my ignorance, and it helped lay out the boundaries of my life.

Arthur Miller

A Community
of Scholars

A university, it is said, is a group of people who have come together to learn from one another. This is an account of one American university, a vast, complicated, rapidly changing institution with 18,000 students and 4,000 teachers who have come together from every section of the country, from 88 other countries, and from every background imaginable.

Universities exist for three reasons: to teach what man knows, to preserve this knowledge for future use, and to create new knowledge. These also were the objectives a thousand years ago when the world's earliest universities began to take shape in Egypt, Italy, and France.

The university described in this book flourishes in the heart of a sprawling city. It consists of 18 separate schools, ranging from a college of arts and sciences,

which resembles many of the small independent colleges, to schools of engineering, fine arts, nursing, law, and veterinary medicine.

Its 18,000 students include 7,000 undergraduates who are working for bachelor's degrees, an equal number of graduate students and students in professional schools who are studying for advanced degrees, and 4,000 men and women who attend part time, often after they have worked all day at a job.

Along with its 18 schools, the university has 26 libraries, including two huge general libraries seven stories high. Together they comprise a vast storehouse of man's knowledge, with over two million books, hundreds of thousands of journals, documents, pamphlets, and maps, and countless microfilms, microcards, computer tapes, and other devices on which information is stored. Much of this knowledge has accumulated over centuries. But far more is the new knowledge, which has been growing at a fantastic rate. It is estimated that man now knows a hundred times more than he did in 1900 and that he will know a thousand times more by the year 2000. To stay abreast of this continuing flood of information, each year the university must add enormous quantities of new material to its collections, including 75,000 books alone.

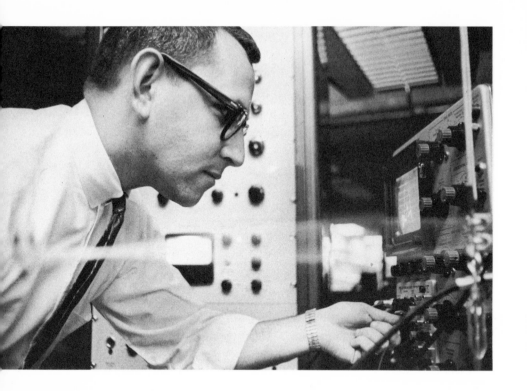

Much of this new knowledge comes from the laboratories, workrooms, and computer centers of the universities themselves. In fact, one of the great changes at universities in recent years has been a dramatic increase in the amount of research they conduct. This has been due in large part to the billions of dollars the Federal government, foundations, and business firms have contributed for studies of importance to them. In the process universities have become major centers for research into some of the nation's most pressing problems.

At this university, faculty members are studying the causes of crime, working toward cures for many diseases, and seeking solutions to many of the problems of the cities and the suburbs. In addition, they are deal-

ing with scores of other matters that affect everyday life. The engineer in the photograph, for example, is conducting a study which may result in more durable bridges, buildings, and airplanes. The woman shown above is trying to find better ways to help children who have trouble reading.

There is also a large amount of research here which is not concerned with solving problems. The objective is simply to learn more about man and his environment. A team of physicists you will read about later has been studying the behavior of an elusive nuclear particle called the K meson. At some point the knowledge they uncover may be "useful," but pursuing what man does not yet know is, they believe, reason enough for such research.

SOURCE: U.S. OFFICE OF EDUCATION

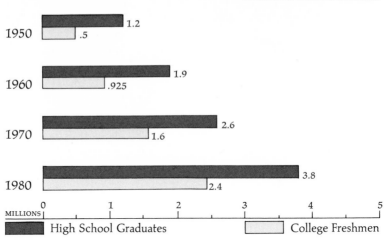

1950 — 1.2 / .5
1960 — 1.9 / .925
1970 — 2.6 / 1.6
1980 — 3.8 / 2.4

MILLIONS: 0 1 2 3 4 5

■ High School Graduates   ☐ College Freshmen

Universities also have been growing larger. The nation's prosperity, the ever-rising need for highly trained specialists, the growing belief that everyone is entitled to a college education have resulted in an enormous increase in the number of young people who attend schools of higher education.

Throughout the country well over half of those who graduate from high school now go on to college. As the graph shows, the number will continue to rise. Enrollment in the graduate and professional schools has also been increasing rapidly. Not too many years ago fewer than 10 per cent of college graduates sought an advanced degree. Now over 25 per cent do. In all, the number of students enrolled in the universities and colleges has climbed from two million in 1950 to over seven million today. By 1980 the number may reach ten million.

This continuing growth has been changing the face of universities and colleges throughout the country. On this campus, enrollment doubled in a ten-year period

14

and has continued to rise. As a result more than thirty new buildings have gone up, many others have been expanded, and still others are being built.

At some state universities there have been so many new students it has been necessary to establish additional campuses in other parts of the state, with the result that these universities have become "multiversities." In other cases hundreds of brand-new schools have been organized. The majority are two-year community colleges which provide all the training some students want and serve as a stepping stone for others who wish to continue their education elsewhere.

As this is written, the number of schools of higher education in the United States has climbed to almost 2,500. Of these only 150 are universities, but they account for half of all the nation's undergraduates and most of those seeking advanced degrees in the graduate and professional schools.

The Students

It is usually in the spring that seniors at high schools and preparatory schools across the country learn if they have been accepted by the universities or colleges to which they have applied. Some have no difficulty in getting into the school they want. But with the intense competition for acceptance, many others find they must settle for a second or a third choice or continue their search. In the end, however, over a million and a half applicants are admitted as members of the freshman class.

The process of finding a school to attend ordinarily starts a full year earlier in the spring of a student's junior year. It is then that young people who plan to go to college meet with their guidance counselors to learn something of the possibilities. Many also do a good deal of research on their own in this period or turn for

Name ......**Galen**.....................**Robert**.....................**David**...................
(Last)   (First)   (Middle)   (Do not use initials)

Home Address ...**1555 Bay Laurel Dr.**.....**Menlo Park**.....**San Mateo**.....**California**.....**94025**..........
(Street Address)   (City)   (County)   (State)   (Zip Code)

Temporary Address ....
(School or other address if not residing at home)   (City)   (County)   (State)   (Zip Code)

Home Telephone Number ...**(415)** **325-5715**...................   Date of Birth: | 1 | 2 | | 1 | 0 | | 4 | 9 |
month   day   year

Please indicate your status:	*Applying for financial aid?*	Yes ☐	No ☒

☒ Regular Freshman

☐ Early Decision Freshman

Does either of your parents hold a Pennsylvania undergraduate degree?   Yes ☐   No ☒

☐ Transfer from another college

☒ Male   ☐ Female

Are you eligible for a Faculty-Staff Scholarship at the University?   Yes ☐   No ☒

Do you wish to live in the University residence halls?   Yes ☒   No ☐

Citizen of the United States?   Yes ☒   No ☐

Please indicate the specific course of study desired. (Check only one)

The College (for men):

  ☐ Arts and Sciences

  ☐ 3/2 Program (Liberal Arts-Engineering)

The Wharton School of Finance & Commerce

  ☒ Bachelor of Science in Economics

The Engineering Schools (4 year Program):

  ☐ Chemical Engineering

  ☐ Civil Engineering

  ☐ Electrical Engineering

  ☐ Mechanical Engineering

  ☐ Metallurgical Engineering

The College of Liberal Arts for Women:

  ☐ Arts and Sciences

  ☐ 3/2 Program (Liberal Arts-Engineering)

  ☐ Elementary or Secondary School Teaching

The School of Allied Medical Professions:

  ☐ Medical Technology (*Not* Pre-Medicine)

  ☐ Occupational Therapy

  ☐ Physical Therapy

The School of Nursing:

  ☐ Four-year Basic Program

List all secondary schools and colleges you have attended and those you plan to attend prior to the expected date of admission. List first the school you are now attending.

OFFICIAL NAME OF INSTITUTIONS	LOCATION (Street Address City and State)	DATE OF ENTERING (Month and Year)	PAST OR EXPECTED DATE OF LEAVING (Month and Year)	DID OR WILL YOU GRADUATE?
Present School				
Menlo-Atherton HS	Middlefield Rd & Ravenswood Ave. Atherton, Calif.	9/64	6/68	yes

advice to placement agencies which specialize in matching students and schools.

During the late spring and summer a great number visit those schools that interest them. Frequently they meet with an admissions officer, as the girl shown on the preceding page is doing, tour the campus, and talk with students.

20

By late fall most have decided which universities or colleges they want to attend. They complete applications, have their schools send in their grades, and if necessary obtain references and attend an interview.

Ordinarily a student also takes a three-hour examination which tests his ability to reason and solve problems. Students have come to regard these tests as so

important that many prepare for them by taking expensive cram courses. But testing officials maintain they are a waste of money. The only practical preparation, they say, is to read widely and study conscientiously over the years and to become familiar with the kinds of questions likely to be asked. Some of these are mathematical problems. Others are multiple-choice questions which concern use of the English language and interpretation of brief essays. The questions below are typical.*

1. Choose the lettered word or phrase which is most nearly *opposite* in meaning to the word in capital letters.
   EXAGGERATION: (A) slight misunderstanding (B) silence (C) accurate representation (D) truth (E) understatement

2. Choose the one word or set of words which, when inserted in the sentence, *best* fits in with the meaning of the sentence as a whole.

   From the first the islanders, despite an outward ————, did what they could to ———— the ruthless occupying force. (A) harmony—assist (B) enmity—embarrass (C) rebellion—foil (D) resistance—destroy (E) acquiescence—thwart

3. Select the lettered pair which best expresses a relationship similar to that expressed in the original pair.
   BICYCLE:LOCOMOTION:

   (A) canoe:paddle (B) hero:worship (C) hay:horse (D) spectacles:vision (E) statement:contention

* Reprinted from "A Description of the College Board Scholastic Aptitude Test" with permission of the College Entrance Examination Board, Princeton, New Jersey.

4. The primary reason for charging lower rates to people who purchase life insurance policies early in life is that this practice

(A) encourages young people to buy policies

(B) recognizes the inability of young people to pay high premiums

(C) reflects the longer period of time during which such people may be expected to pay premiums

(D) reflects the high percentage of insurance sales made to people between the ages of twenty and thirty

(E) reflects the increase in life expectancy

5. A line segment is drawn from the point (0,0) to the point (6,4). What are the coordinates of the midpoint?

(A) (2,3) (B) (3,2) (c) (3,4) (D) (6,2) (E) (12,8)

6. The cost of electrical energy in a certain area is as follows:

	Cents per kilowatt-hour
First 100 kilowatt-hours	3
Second 100 kilowatt-hours	2.5
Third 100 kilowatt-hours	2

How many kilowatt-hours can one obtain for $5?

(A) 175 (B) 180 (c) 200 (D) 225 (E) 250

7. Which of the following statements must be false if
   A > B and B > C?

   I. $B + C > A$
   II. $2C > A + B$
   III. $A + B > A + C$
   IV. $A + C > B + C$

(A) None (B) I only (c) II only (D) I and II only
(E) I, II, III, and IV *

* The answers to these questions are as follows:
1, E; 2, E; 3, D; 4, C; 5, B; 6, B; 7, C.

By January all the information a school needs usually has been assembled and the admissions staff begins making its decisions. At the university we are concerned with, the task involves selecting a freshman class of 1,700 men and women from more than 8,000 applicants.

A student's academic record and his test scores are, of course, of great importance in reaching a decision. His extracurricular activities also have some weight. But often a decision is influenced by other factors as well.

A student receives additional consideration at this school, for example, if he has worked hard to achieve an important goal, such as attending special classes every summer because of his interest in becoming a doctor, or holding a job to pay for music lessions. This also is the case if he has achieved a good academic record despite a serious handicap.

An applicant's background is also of considerable importance. A great many undergraduates here have essentially the same background: they are white, have college-educated parents, and have been raised in comfortable suburban homes. The objective, however, is to have students from all walks of life who bring to the campus a diversity of experience and viewpoints.

As a result, a boy from a farm, a mining district, or a fishing village whose family has a low income has a better chance of being admitted than a boy who is equally bright but lives in a suburb. The same preference is given to city dwellers, particularly black students from ghetto communities.

However, when this was written, only 200 of the 6,800 undergraduates here were Negroes, a situation similar to that at many schools. Throughout the nation, in fact, fewer than 5 per cent of the college-age Negroes attend college. A lack of money and the poor preparation that many ghetto schools provide are two of the reasons for this. But the universities also have been responsible. Out of prejudice or nearsightedness, over the years many have not been willing to admit any more than a token number of Negroes and these were usually from well-educated, well-to-do families.

In response to a changing climate in this country, however, universities now are actively seeking Negroes for their student bodies. At this university a Negro admissions officer has been hired to recruit black students, and black students already on campus have been asked to help. In addition, a more flexible admissions policy has been adopted which takes into account the poor

schooling that handicaps many such students. Of course, what will come of these efforts remains to be seen.

There also are several groups that traditionally receive special consideration here and at other universities. They include children of the alumni, the faculty, and the university staff, and young people recommended by trustees or wealthy alumni. The fact that a student is an excellent athlete also carries a good deal of weight. In fact, eighty-five places are set aside each year in the freshman class for athletes whose academic records do not meet the standards for others who apply.

Each application is evaluated by one of the admissions officers, then reviewed by the dean or vice-dean of admissions. By early spring they have made their choices and letters have been sent to each applicant. Most start, "Regretfully I must inform you that the Committee on Admissions has been unable to approve your application. . . ." The others, however, bear good news. "You have been accepted," they read. "Undergraduates, teachers, and alumni look forward to your association with . . . (the) university."

Getting into a good school is an important achievement. But even after this hurdle there remains another for many students and their parents. It is paying the expenses involved. Tuition and other costs of an education have been rising steadily and the likelihood is that they will continue to do so.

As this is written, the overall cost of attending a public school, such as a state university, is about $1,600 a year. This includes tuition, fees, books, equipment, room, board, clothing, and personal expenses. The cost of attending a private university or college now averages $2,700 a year and at many schools is far higher. At the one we are concerned with, it is $3,700 a year. Even a student who lives at home and attends a school that does not charge tuition can count on spending almost $1,000 each year on books, supplies, clothing, and transportation.

Not too long ago a determined student could pay all his expenses with what he earned at jobs during the school year and the summer. But the cost of an education today is so high that this is an unusual achievement.

The objective at this school and at a growing number of others is to make it possible for every student who is admitted to attend whether or not he has the money to do so. This university first decides how much a family can afford to contribute, based on its financial situation and on what a student can be expected to earn during the summer. It then tries to provide what is lacking.

Each year it distributes over 12 million dollars in aid which takes the form of jobs, loans, and/or scholarship grants. About half the students here receive help, including some from families with annual incomes as high as $16,000. One undergraduate in four, for example, is given a part-time job on campus which involves working 10 hours a week. The jobs include serving food or washing dishes in the dining halls, sorting dirty laundry in the dormitories, as the students on page 28 are doing, selling sandwiches and snacks at night, and assisting faculty members. Many students also are given loans, at a low 3 per cent interest rate, which they do not have to pay back until after they graduate and hold full-time jobs. In addition, a sizable number are awarded grants which do not have to be repaid.

At many schools, however, there is not enough money available to assist everyone who needs help, even with the large sums the Federal government has been contributing for this purpose. In such cases, of course, it is the students with the highest grades and the lowest family incomes who have the best chance of receiving help. Often athletes also receive special consideration.

If a student is denied financial aid at his school, he still may be able to win a scholarship or a loan from a government agency or some other organization. However, frequently his parents must provide most or all of what is needed. If they do not have the money, some borrow from a bank and also cut corners at home. In other cases a mother may go to work. But somehow the money is usually raised.

The first weeks at this university are likely to be among the most trying a student will experience in all the years he spends here. Freshmen arrive plagued by confusion, homesickness, and a great many questions only time can answer. They wonder if they really will be able to do the work, if people will like them, if they will like their roommates, if life will be stimulating, if they will change.

Meanwhile, there is also the problem of adjusting to a highly complicated place. Although it is a problem the student must solve for himself, the university does what it can to help. In each freshman dormitory there are several counselors, either seniors or graduate students, whose job it is to make the new students feel at home. Each freshman girl also has an older student or "big sister" she can turn to. In addition, there are

three wildly busy days before classes start which are
known as Freshman Week.

In this period students meet with their faculty advisors, attend panel discussions on student life, hear about
traditions and extracurricular activities, learn school
songs such as the "Red and Blue," * try out for crew,

* "Come all ye loyal classmen now/In hall and campus through/Lift
up your hearts and voices/For the royal Red and Blue. . . ."

football, soccer, and other sports, and, if they aren't too tired, go downtown to look around.

They also are tested and have their pictures taken. The test they are taking here tells how effectively they read. Others are concerned with their physical condition, with how well they swim, and, if they are business majors, with their aptitude for accounting. The picture is for their records.

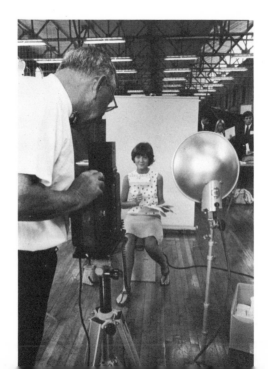

Each night, in addition, there is a party or a picnic to help students meet other students.

Meanwhile many new students from countries throughout the world also have arrived on campus. Together with those who are continuing their studies, there are more than twelve hundred foreign students here, most of whom are enrolled in the graduate and professional schools.

The adjustment they must make is, of course, far more difficult than it is for any American student. Many must learn English as well as the techniques of studying at what for them is a foreign university. They also must learn how things are done in this country, such as how to board a bus, use a telephone, shop at

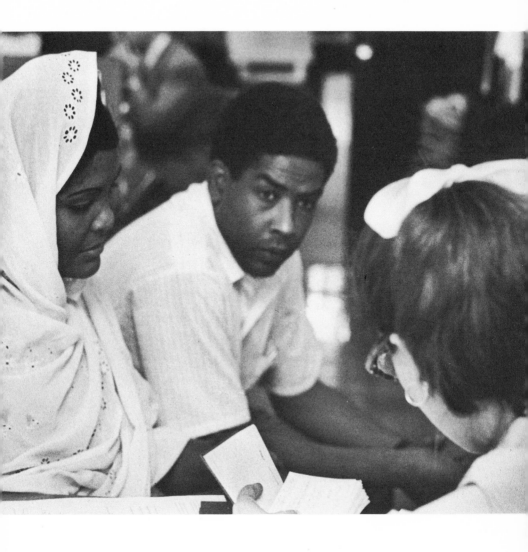

a supermarket, or entertain. Some who are married bring their wives and children, but most, because of the high costs, leave their families behind and live as bachelors for the years they spend here.

To make things easier for new foreign students, those already established at the university serve as advisors and guides. So do a number of American students and many local families.

By the last day of Freshman Week, there remains only the need to register for courses, buy textbooks, and await the start of classes.

There are two thousand undergraduate courses in over sixty different subjects offered at this university. Each course meets at least three hours a week for fourteen weeks, or one semester. Some also involve additional time in laboratories or recitation sections. To obtain a bachelor's degree here it is necessary to pass forty such courses, usually five each semester.

These include sixteen that are required: two in English, two in a foreign language, four in science and mathematics, four in the social sciences, and four in philosophy, music, art, or the other humanities. In addition, each student must take a minimum of twelve courses in his major subject and at least another ten as electives in any fields he chooses. He also must complete two semesters of physical education.

Some students are able to skip one or two of the introductory courses because of work they took in high school. If they pass an examination they may take advanced work in that field at the outset. During his first semester one freshman took the schedule of courses shown on the next page. It includes introductory biology, anthropology, and prose, advanced French, economic theory, and physical education.

A freshman soon finds that one of the most important differences between attending a high school and a university is what is expected of him. At a university there is far more reading and other preparation, perhaps twice as much, but there also is far more freedom.

In high school a student's teachers, and often his parents, were forever checking to see that he had done the work. At a university he is largely on his own. A professor will explain the material and convey as best he can its significance and excitement. But whether a student pays attention, does the assignments, studies

	Monday	Tuesday	Wednesday	Thursday	Friday
8		French		French	
9	Anthropology (Lecture)		Anthropology (Lecture)		
10	Physical Education		Physical Education		Physical Education
11					
12	English	Biology (Lecture)	English	Biology (Lecture)	English
1	Economics		Economics		Economics
2	Biology (Laboratory)				
3			Anthropology (Recitation)		
4					
5					

for examinations, or even attends his classes is up to him.

Another difference is in the size of the classes. Many are far larger than any in high school, which leaves little opportunity for questions or discussion. This is particularly true of the introductory courses freshmen must take, such as those in biology, psychology, mathematics, and French.

There are, for example, more than six hundred students enrolled in the introductory biology course here. They meet twice a week in the vast gloomy auditorium shown above for lectures by a full professor of biology. At this session he is discussing the nephron of the kidney.

Once a week they also meet in twenty-six separate sections for their laboratory work. Each section is taught by a graduate student who is working for his Ph.D. in biology. The system is essentially the same in other introductory courses. A professor gives the lectures. A graduate student conducts each of the laboratory or recitation sections, where the ideas presented in the lectures are discussed and there is an opportunity to ask questions.

Some graduate students are very good teachers, making up in enthusiasm what they lack in experience. But others, students will tell you, are dreadful. Officials of the university are the first to admit that this is not an ideal arrangement. But they say there are so many students signed up for the introductory courses that there are not enough professors to teach them all.

By his sophomore year a student's lot improves. His lecture courses are more like the one above in Marxist and Socialist thought. There also are a number of small seminars available, such as the one shown below in Negro history, where the emphasis is on exploring ideas and exchanging viewpoints.

When the weather is good, moreover, there are professors who prefer to do their teaching out-of-doors.

Some members of the faculty genuinely enjoy teaching. They also find it helps them learn. As one professor explained, "I am continually being excited by things that come up in class that I hadn't thought about before."

There are others, however, who see teaching only as a necessary chore which takes time from research or scholarship. In fact some come to the university only on the condition that they will not have to teach freshmen, and others insist that they teach only graduate students.

Unlike some universities, however, everyone on the

40

faculty here does teach and eventually develops a reputation among the students as to how good a teacher he is. This is reported in detail each year in the student newspaper's *Course Guide*, a 160-page book based on an annual survey of student opinion.

Some teachers get very high grades, such as Alexander V. Riasonovsky, a "dynamic showman" who offers a "superb" course in Russian history, and Cirriaco Arroyo, "the hottest property" in the Spanish Department. But not all are so popular. A teacher of a Shakespeare course is taken to task for her "incredible incompetence." So is a professor of anthropology for his "boring lectures . . . delivered in a monotonous drone."

For some students one of the frustrations of attending a large university is the difficulty they have in getting to know members of the faculty on a personal basis. They come to the campus with the expectation that at times they will sit with their teachers over coffee, lunch, or beer and discuss important issues and that they even may be invited to their homes. Although this may be the case at smaller schools, it usually is not at large universities. Often the closest contact a new student may have with his professors is what he sees of them from a seat in a lecture hall.

One reason for this is that faculty members are busy. Their research, their work with graduate students, and their other duties do not leave them a great deal of time. Another reason is that many teachers, although not all, have no interest in getting to know their younger students on a personal basis. A history professor had this to say. "The kind of relationship students want with the faculty is between pupil and guru. They

41

want to sit at my feet and listen to my wise words, or they want to be my buddy. In my free time I don't want to be a guru or a buddy. I want to be with people who share my interests and most undergraduates I meet don't."

It is also true, however, that many new students are shy and despite their desire do not make very much of an effort to meet their teachers. Each faculty member, for example, is required to set aside office hours when his students can meet with him, as the student above is doing with his English teacher. But few students appear. There also are coffee hours the university sponsors each week for faculty and students. But more often than not the students talk among themselves and the faculty members drink their coffee and depart.

A freshman explained it this way. "You see a teacher you have and it's very possible that you can go over and talk with him. But you have this feeling that he doesn't know who you are, or even if he does that he's not interested in talking to you."

Yet officials at the university feel that teachers and students, particularly freshmen, would benefit from seeing somewhat more of one another. As a result, the freshmen have dinner each week with their faculty advisors. In addition, every freshman receives an invitation from the university chaplain or one of the deans to a supper party at his house. Usually a teacher or a member of the university staff is invited as a speaker. At the party shown above the speaker was the dean of women.

How difficult is the first year? At this university it is common to hear freshmen complain, particularly in the first weeks, that the beginning courses are no more challenging than those they took as high school seniors. The differences, they say, are in the quality of the students, the amount of homework, and the competition for grades.

As students, freshmen seem to fall into several categories. Just as in high school, some do little or no work. Others cram their studying into periods just before examinations. Others regularly spend three or four hours a night studying. Still others, known locally as worms, do little else but study.

The results of the first hourly examinations usually bring about some changes. Students do not complain as much about how easy the courses are. Also, the number of worms increases dramatically.

One of the problems that plagues freshmen is setting aside enough time to study, then disciplining themselves to use it for that purpose. At times it is a question

44

of learning to use the freedom one suddenly has acquired. However, the problem also may be a symptom of "freshman slump." After four years of working hard to get into a college, it is difficult for some students to "build up steam" to run still another race.

Another problem is finding a place to study. At the outset many students try studying in their dormitory rooms, but frequently there are too many distractions. For some the library is a solution, although at night it often is a better place to meet members of the opposite sex than it is to study. For others what works best is an empty classroom or an unused office or a place deep in the library stacks where they can be totally alone.

DEPARTMENT	COURSE NO	COURSE DESCRIPTION	CREDIT	GRADE
ENGL	101	PROSE	1#	B
MATH	140	CALCULUS I	1#	B
PH ED		PHYSICAL EDUCATION	0#	B
REL T	3	LIVING REL – FAR EAST	1#	C
SOC	1	INTRO TO SOCIOLOGY	1#	A
SPAN	3	INTERMED SPANISH	1#	C
		TERM AVERAGE 2.80		

At the end of the semester each student receives his grades in the mail. Two out of three will do reasonably well, but others may receive a distinct shock. Either they have failed a course or their overall grades are so low they have been placed on probation. In the case of freshmen this requires a D-plus average. A student who does this poorly must improve his record enough to be taken off probation the next semester, or he is asked to leave the university.

What one learns from a teacher, a laboratory experiment, or a book is, of course, only part of what there is to be learned at a university. Of equal importance is what a student learns about himself and others. Often for the first time he must make all the decisions that affect his life, deciding what he does not because somebody says it is right but for reasons he can support inside himself.

There are decisions regarding behavior. Is it right,

for example, to drink, to use drugs, as a third of the students here claim to do, or, if one is single, to have sexual relations?

There are decisions regarding one's beliefs in politics, religion, the role of government, the morality of business, and other issues. Some young people have strong beliefs about such matters, but others may bring with them ideas that merely reflect those of their parents. Now these ideas are challenged by students or teachers who see things in a different way. Who is right? What should they believe?

There also are decisions regarding goals. It is easy enough in high school to see the need for a college edu-

cation. But when a student finally enters a university things become more complicated. As his experience broadens, he may puzzle over what kind of a person he wants to be, what he really wants from life, whether his education is helping him, whether indeed he would be better off doing something else.

If he finds answers often they are rooted in the relationships he develops, such as those with his roommates, who usually are willing to talk far into the night about such matters, and those with students he dates. Although much of the dating here is casual, sometimes it results in serious friendships, which inevitably raises still other questions.

48

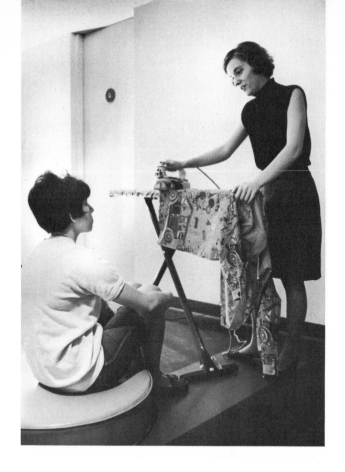

During the first months at a university, however, one of the most important persons in a freshman's life may be a dormitory counselor. There are over a hundred who live in the freshman dormitories. Their job, as noted earlier, is to help students adjust to college. Sometimes all that is needed is information on what to wear on a particular occasion. But when a student is homesick or problems arise with school work, roommates, or parents, often there is a need to talk things over. When a problem is serious enough a counselor may send a student to one of the university's counseling services which help with emotional problems, with reading and studying, and with other difficulties.

The campus organizations a student joins also may have an important influence on his life. This is particularly true of the thirty-three fraternities and ten sororities here whose members live together, eat together, attend the same parties, wear jeweled membership pins, participate in secret rituals, and to a considerable extent occupy a world of their own. Over 2,500 students, or one undergraduate in three, are members of these groups.

Each year several weeks are set aside as a "rushing" period during which new students visit those fraternity or sorority houses they think they might like to join. At the same time the "brothers" and "sisters" at these houses have a chance to look over the new crop of freshmen and decide which ones they might like to have as members. These students then are invited back for various events so that the members can get to know them better. Finally, the house decides which of these it wants and bids to join are issued.

The students who accept become pledges who must

endure a series of tests and trials before they can be initiated as members and move out of their dormitories into their new houses.

There are many advantages to joining a fraternity or a sorority. The meals and living conditions are better than those the university provides and the cost is not much higher. A freshman also finds acceptance in a closely-knit group, which can be helpful on a large, impersonal campus where loneliness often is a problem

for a new student. In addition, the fraternities dominate the social life with the lively parties they hold on weekends, which not only are fun but make it easier for their members to meet girls.

However, these organizations come in for a good deal of criticism. Traditionally most have practiced religious and racial discrimination, limiting their membership to white Protestants, white Catholics, or Jews. Usually this has been in line with the rules of their national organizations. In recent years many such groups have liberalized these rules in response to pressures from students and from schools that threatened to ban them. As a result, they now permit their chapters to select members on the basis of character alone.

But even with this change discrimination persists in fraternities and sororities here and elsewhere. In large part it is perpetuated by bigoted or thoughtless students, although the indifference of university officials also plays a role. There are a few fraternities on campus that freely accept members of any religion or race, but many admit only a token number and others continue to admit only "their kind." During the rushing period, in fact, many freshmen already know enough to ask which houses are "Christian" and which are "Jewish." Moreover, anyone can tell them.

Fraternities also are criticized on two other counts. One relates to schoolwork. With the emphasis they place on having a good time, they are said to have a bad effect on the grades of their members. For years the grades of fraternity men at this university have lagged behind those of students who did not join. However, the fraternities have been trying to change this. Some now have formal study hours; others require pledges to study under supervision for several hours a night. As a result of such efforts, grades have risen, although generally they remain below those of other students.

Fraternities also have been criticized for hazing, a process designed to test the desire of a pledge to become a member. For example, a pledge may be required to wear a costume in public, wear a ludicrous sign on his back, or push a peanut along a street with his nose.

Hazing also may involve physical hardship. On a few campuses, in fact, it has resulted in injury and even in death. Although such misfortunes have not occurred here, pledges have been branded with razor blades and hot pins, made to walk in circles for hours on end, and struck repeatedly with wooden paddles.

In a recent year fraternity leaders at the university vowed to do away with hazing. Instead the emphasis

53

was placed on useful works, a policy the sororities traditionally have followed. Pledges collected for charities and cleaned vacant lots in slum areas. As in the past, they also performed chores around their house, as those shown above are doing.

But the change apparently did not extend to Hell Weekend, the last hurdle before membership is granted. At one fraternity house, for example, members stripped pledges of their clothing, poured molasses and cornflakes on their bodies, forced them to eat raw eggs, raw onions, and dog food, made them crawl along a slime-covered floor, then placed them under icy showers where they were required to perform sit-ups, push-ups, and squat thrusts until they were too tired to go on. Having come through this ordeal a pledge earned the right to be called "brother."

Brother is also a term the black students at this pre-dominantly white university use in addressing one another. However, it has a deeper meaning for them. For years there were only a handful of Negroes on this campus, usually from highly-educated, well-to-do families. When they arrived they tried hard to make a place for themselves in the student community.

But as the number of black students here has slowly increased and more have come from urban ghettos, this has changed. Although these students have a deep interest in the education available to them, many have little interest in the white students and their activities. They say they are not comfortable in a white world they feel is insensitive to the needs of Negroes. The result has been that they keep to themselves in a tightly-knit community, as is the case on many campuses. Few attend "white" parties and few date white students. Although a number now are asked to join the fraternities, few accept. The year this was written only five Negroes were members. "I'd rather not be the house nigger," one student explained. Instead he joined an all-black fraternity at another university nearby.

Many of the black students here also do not participate in extracurricular activities. The only exception is SAAS, the Society for African and Afro-American Students, an organization which works to improve conditions for Negroes at the university. Black students at other schools have formed similar groups.

SAAS has been at least partly responsible for several important changes here. These include an increase in the number of black students admitted each year, the employment of a Negro admissions officer, and the establishment of a course in Negro history. It also has helped bring about an increase in the number of black persons the university hires for jobs. When the Negro leader Martin Luther King was assassinated, SAAS also organized the procession shown below. Almost every

black student at the university participated, mournfully singing protest songs as they moved slowly through the campus. Almost a thousand white students silently followed.

The changes that SAAS helped bring about were not isolated achievements. They reflected a widespread change which has seen a growing number of schools give their students a voice in determining policies that affect them.

One reason officials have taken this step is a belief that today's students, unlike those in the past, have the maturity and background for this responsibility. On many campuses, however, student protests also have been an important factor.

Frequently these protests have focused on the rules that regulate student life. Unlike schools in other countries, those in the United States have traditionally served as substitute parents, deciding where students must live, whether members of the opposite sex may visit them in their rooms, at what time women must be in their dormitories at night, and even where students must eat. Arguing that they are young adults, not children, students have asked that these rules be eliminated or liberalized.

They also have protested against other policies and approaches at their schools, such as those that permit discrimination by fraternities, or ignore the needs of poor people in neighboring ghettos, or support the nation's military efforts.

The students who participate in such protests have come to be known as "activists." Although only a small number are usually involved, they are likely to include some of the best students. At times other students disagree with the activists on an issue and conduct demonstrations of their own. But most go quietly about their business.

The activists have used a wide range of techniques to dramatize their complaints. They have passed out literature, organized rallies, picketed, and conducted "sit-ins" and "sleep-ins" in school buildings. On a number of campuses, as noted earlier, feelings became so bitter that students took over buildings, damaged property, and even held officials as hostages, tactics that led to arrests and more bitterness.

Activists on this campus have been concerned primarily with the university's role in military affairs. One target was a research project relating to germ warfare which scientists here were conducting for the Department of Defense. The students objected for two reasons. They regarded germ warfare as immoral. Moreover, the project was secret and therefore violated a university policy which prohibits research that cannot be made public. When the research continued after repeated complaints, a group of sixty students decided to demonstrate. For three days and two nights they sat in the corridors of venerable College Hall, where the president of the university has his office. Their protest triggered a formal request from the faculty that the project be removed, to which the university finally agreed.

Activists here also have tried to change a policy which permits the armed forces and weapons manufacturers to visit the campus to recruit students for jobs. One year the Dow Chemical Company was the target of these protests, as it was on campuses throughout the country.

Whenever a Dow recruiter visited the campus, the activists organized a demonstration. At one point they even occupied the office in which he planned to conduct his interviews. The dean of men, shown at the right in the photograph, is asking them to leave. Although the students demonstrated against Dow again and again that year, the university would not change its policy.

Most activists demonstrate because they feel a strong ethical obligation to try to change a policy with which they disagree. Of course, in demonstrating they exercise an ancient right to dissent that each of us has. Through their efforts, moreover, they frequently have helped bring about desirable changes.

On the other hand, serious questions have been raised by the tactics that some activists have used. Is it right, for example, for students to so badly disrupt a school that those who wish to attend classes cannot do so? In addition, are students justified in damaging property, holding officials hostage, or breaking the law in other ways to achieve their goals?

Just how much influence students now have in the affairs of their schools varies a great deal. At a few schools little has changed. At many, officials continue to make their own decisions but pay far more attention than they once did to what students think. At others, students now serve with administrators and teachers on committees that help make academic and social policies.

Where students have gained a voice, often there have been important changes. At many schools, including this university, social rules have been liberalized. At some, admissions procedures, courses, and methods of grading also have been changed. In addition, secret military research on university campuses has all but disappeared.

Social and academic affairs on this campus are supervised by a platoon of deans and assistant deans. But many aspects of student life are regulated by the students themselves through a Student Government.

It consists of an Assembly the students elect, which is shown at one of its weekly meetings, a fraternity council, a sorority council, and a system of courts where students accused of breaking campus rules are tried.

One of the Assembly's major jobs is solving problems that confront the student body. It isn't always successful, but twice in recent years it has had major accomplishments. One was the establishment of parietal hours, periods during which a student may entertain a member of the opposite sex in his room.

What led to this change was a need students felt for greater privacy. Although they could have guests in

the living rooms of their dormitories, often it was difficult for a young man and a young woman to find a
place where they could be alone. The Assembly pro-
posed its solution and the university agreed.

The university also adopted many recommendations
of a Student Government committee that spent fifteen
months studying ways of strengthening the education
offered here. One change involved a student's major
subject. Previously it had been necessary to major in
an established field of study. Now, if approval is granted,
a student may develop his own major, drawing on
courses from throughout the university.

In addition, a "pass-fail" system was adopted. Formerly students were often reluctant to take elective courses that interested them if they were outside their major fields because of the risk of a low grade. Now if a student passes such a course his record shows only that he has passed, no matter how low a grade he receives. Of course, if he fails, it shows that too.

The Assembly also has responsibility for disbursing almost $200,000 in student fees to campus organizations. It not only decides which are eligible but how much they should get.

At times it organizes activities on its own when there seems to be a need. One of its most ambitious projects has been a Free University, which offers off-beat courses that otherwise would not be available here. These have ranged from *Self-Hypnosis* to *Practical Politics* and *Biology for Poets*. Faculty members and students serve as teachers, and anyone from the university or the community may enroll free of charge.

The courts the Student Government operates are conducted by panels of student judges. There are male judges for men students and female judges for women. The charges in the cases they hear are brought by university officials, teachers, and students. They range from disorderly conduct in a dormitory to cheating, drinking, or gambling.* Women also may be tried for leaving their dormitories at night without signing out, or returning after their curfew, which is 1:30 A.M. on weekdays and 2:15 A.M. on weekends.

A student's first offense will often result in a warning. In a case of cheating, however, a court may recommend

* A student may be charged with drinking if legally he is too young to drink or if he is drinking in an area where it is not permitted. At fraternity parties, however, the rule regarding age is not enforced.

64

that a student be given a failure. With a curfew violation, the penalty usually is a restriction to the campus
for several nights, or "campusing" as it is known. In
every case a jury also may impose more severe pen-
alties, including a recommendation that a student be
suspended or expelled.

The most serious charges, such as those involving
theft, injury, or the sale or use of drugs, are heard by
the Committee on Student Discipline, which consists
of teachers, university officials and students.

The committee is one of several on which students
now serve with faculty members and administrators.
Others are concerned with the curriculum, student
affairs, and student housing. There also is a group of

forty leading students, teachers, and officials, including the university president, who meet regularly to exchange ideas on problems that confront the school, from its admissions policies to its relationships with the ghetto nearby, matters that not too long ago were not regarded as a proper concern of students.

Students are involved in a bewildering array of other activities. There are in all more than a hundred organizations on this campus that offer a student a chance to pursue his interests. They include a daily newspaper with a staff of 85, an annual budget of $80,000, and a circulation of 10,000 . . .

a radio station that broadcasts music, news, and special
events all day and much of the night, a variety of glee
clubs, orchestras, and bands, a film society that creates
its own movies . . .

and Mask and Wig, a men's dramatic group that each year produces a musical comedy in which men take the roles of women. When its campus performances are over, the show goes on the road so that alumni may see it.

There also are students who spend their free time working to change conditions outside the university. Many spend several hours a week in the neighboring ghettos in projects organized by the Community Involvement Council, the largest student group on campus.

The student above is one of many who have tutored local children in their school work or trained older children to serve as tutors. Students also have helped with recreation programs, voter education, discussion groups for young mothers, and problems that arise when people must move because of urban renewal.

Meanwhile, hundreds of others have turned to politics, joining students throughout the country in efforts to elect those candidates whose views on war, peace, the cities, and other issues resemble theirs.

There also are students who speak their minds in other ways, using as a forum the countless fences that come and go as new buildings rise.

EXISTENCE EXIST

IF IT DOES NOT, NEITHER DO YOU

Athletics also have an important role in this university. Almost half the undergraduates play on dormitory or fraternity teams in an intramural program. There is, however, even greater emphasis on intercollegiate competition. About eight hundred men, including many freshmen, compete in sixteen different sports against schools all over the country.

With a program this size, the Department of Intercollegiate Athletics is one of the largest at the university. It has thirty coaches, four trainers, a sports publicity staff, business and equipment managers, and other specialists. In addition, it operates a 60,000-seat stadium, a 9,000-seat basketball arena, a field house, a boat house, squash and tennis courts, and a training house where athletes take their meals and where they sleep the night before big games.

Although these facilities are impressive, they are no different from those at many other universities. The objective here is also the same. It is to produce as many winning teams as possible. Winning teams require good players, however, and if left to chance it is likely that not enough would enroll at any one school. Therefore coaches may spend much of their time searching the high schools and preparatory schools for promising athletes. When they find one they do everything they can to convince him to enroll.

The head football coach at this university writes each year to football coaches at 3,600 secondary schools asking for their recommendations. He also relies on reports from a network of alumni who recommend athletes in their areas. When the admissions officers have determined which of these boys meet the academic

standards for athletes, a coach sees each of them in action. Then the Department of Intercollegiate Athletics begins courting those boys it wants.

To start, alumni in their areas entertain them. In addition, they are brought to the university with their parents, where they are shown the campus, introduced to high officials and faculty members, and entertained. Meanwhile, a coach tries to sell them on the advantages of enrolling.

At a number of universities academic standards are lowered sharply to enable athletes with limited scholastic ability to attend. Moreover, they are permitted to take the simplest courses, and everything is done to get them through. In such cases they are, of course, athletes first and students second. Frequently they have their expenses paid, are given fifteen dollars a month for "laundry money," and are guaranteed good jobs for the summer. If many schools are after them, they may be offered more "laundry money," as well as gifts and other inducements. The recruiters at one school, in fact, honor the athletes they want most with a parade.

At this university the academic standards are higher than at many and the financial inducements are not as great, which makes it more difficult for coaches to at-tract players. The policy here, as noted earlier, is that up to eighty-five athletes with lower grades than other students may be admitted each year; however, once they are admitted they are expected to meet the same stand-

ards or they are dropped. If an athlete is in need of financial help, he is offered a scholarship and perhaps a part-time job, just as other students are.

A student who plays on a team here commits himself to a heavy schedule. Not only must he work as hard on his courses as any other student, he must spend as much as forty hours a week on his sport during the season in which it is played.

Football players, in fact, return to the university a full week earlier than other students to attend pre-season practice. When classes begin they spend every afternoon from 3:30 to 6:30 at practice. Afterward they eat at the training house, then finally turn to their studies. If there is a game at home on Saturday they spend Friday night in the training house. If there is a game at a distant school, they may spend the entire weekend away.

Despite its long history and its popularity, intercollegiate athletics is strongly criticized by many educators. What concerns them are the recruitment of the players, the special treatment they are given, the large coaching staffs, and the elaborate facilities, all of which they feel serve no educational purpose. At best, they argue, such a program provides recreation for a small number of students and entertainment for sports fans.

Of course, the coaches disagree. Playing in vigorous competition, they say, builds a student's character. He learns to make sacrifices, to think of his team first, and to win or lose gracefully. They also point out that a winning team strengthens a university by creating a sense of pride among students.

There are two other benefits school officials do not overlook. A team that wins consistently may attract large crowds whose admission fees help pay some of

the costs of running the school. In addition, a winning team may encourage alumni to make financial contributions.

Why are the players willing to spend so much time on athletics? For some, who lack the grades and the money, it provides a chance for a college education. However, most also love to play. As one explained: "When I get a football in my hands, it's me against the other guy. Either he's going to bring me down or I'm going to score. The challenge is always there."

Over a hundred women at the university also compete against other schools in sports such as field hockey, lacrosse, badminton, and softball. Alas, no one comes to see them play.

When a student isn't in class or isn't involved in some activity or isn't studying or isn't asleep, there is a good chance that he is in the Dirty Drug, a luncheonette near the girls' dormitories known for its large, noisy crowds, or at Smokey Joe's, a beer parlor so dark it is almost impossible to see one's companion . . .

or at the Catacombs, a student-run coffeehouse in the basement of the Christian Association where students not only drink coffee but entertain.

On weekends there are parties at fraternity houses, in dormitories, and at the apartments of older students who live off campus. Two or three times a year ordinary weekends grow into big weekends with a football game or a crew race, a concert by a famous entertainer, and more parties than usual. On such occasions many students bring dates from other schools or from home.

One of the biggest of these weekends is called Skimmer. It takes place in the spring just before final examinations. Along with the standard activities, thousands

of students journey to the banks of a nearby river where they picnic, drink, throw their companions in the water, play guitars, kiss their dates, and, possibly, watch the crew go by.

For many years a bachelor's degree was all a college student needed to make his way in the world. But in a growing number of professions this is no longer the case. To perform effectively, and to get ahead, often it is necessary to have even more training. As a result, many students go on to graduate school where they seek either a master's degree, which is one level above the bachelor's, or a doctor of philosophy degree—the Ph.D.—which is the highest degree awarded.

The number of graduate students in this country has been rising rapidly. As this is written, there are more than 700,000, over twice the enrollment ten years ago. This growth is due in large part to the efforts of the Federal government. One of its objectives has been to increase the number of scientists and the amount of scientific research. Another has been to increase the number of college teachers and other professionals in short supply. To meet these objectives it has given the universities huge sums for scholarships, classrooms, buildings, and laboratories.

At this university there are over five thousand graduate students—almost as many as the number of undergraduates. They differ from undergraduates in a variety of ways. They are older, many are married and have a child, such as the architecture student shown below, and most are deeply committed to a particular profession. They also find themselves working far harder than they ever did before.

Frequently the major problem is not the work, but a lack of money. The solution is often a teaching or research fellowship. This university grants about a thousand each year which cover the cost of tuition and

provide three thousand dollars for living expenses. Even with this income, it may be hard for a family to make ends meet. As a result a student's wife may have to go to work, often at a job the university provides, or his parents may have to make a contribution.

In return for the university's help, a teaching fellow conducts two sections of one of the freshman courses. The graduate student above, for example, is teaching a basic course in accounting. He spends from twenty to thirty hours a week preparing for classes and marking papers, which is one reason it takes some graduate students so long to obtain a degree.

The lot of the research fellow is somewhat easier. His job is to help a faculty member in his department carry out a major research project. This physical chemistry student, for example, is one of a team of research fellows who are assisting in a study of unstable molecules. In the process the student is also conducting the necessary research to obtain his degree.

Most of the graduate students in this university, including those in the city-planning class above, are working for a master's degree. Usually this involves taking courses for from one to three years and preparing a long research paper, or thesis. Each year almost fifteen hundred students at the university meet these requirements. But in some cases the requirements are

quite different. This art student, for example, does not attend classes, nor does he receive grades. His degree is awarded when his teachers feel he is ready to pursue a career on his own.

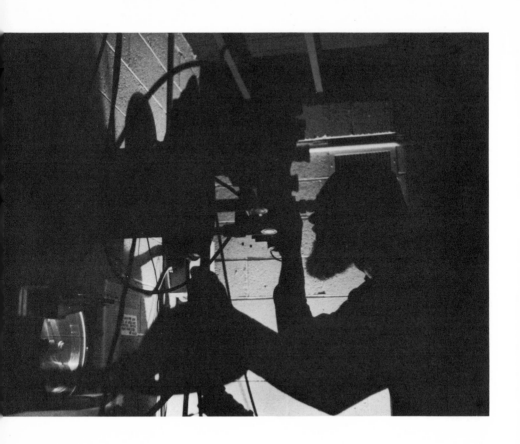

The astronomy student shown above is seeking a Ph.D. which will enable him to teach at a university or serve as a highly-paid researcher for a company or the government. However, the process of earning this degree involves so many hurdles and takes so long that few Ph.D.s are granted. At this university only 275 students received the degree in a recent year. Throughout the country it was less than 20,000.

Obtaining a Ph.D. ordinarily takes from three to six years, but it has been known to take far longer. First, a series of courses must be completed. Then a candidate is tested on what he has learned by a board of faculty members. Usually he also must pass one or

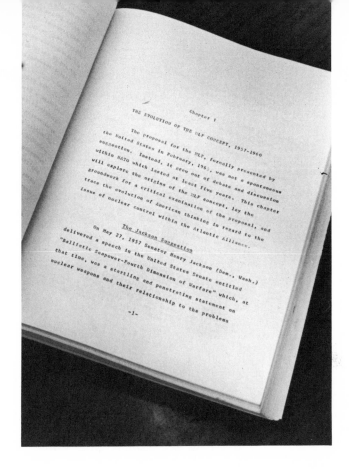

more examinations which test his ability to read foreign languages.

If he qualifies he begins work on a major research project through which he must make an original contribution to man's knowledge. When his research is finished, he presents his findings and conclusions in a report called a doctoral dissertation which frequently is longer than this book. The one shown above deals with the control of nuclear weapons. If the dissertation is approved, it is bound and given a permanent place in the university library. Of even more importance, the student finally is awarded his degree and henceforth may call himself "doctor."

At this university there are also four professional schools with over two thousand students who are preparing to be doctors, dentists, veterinarians, or lawyers.

The medical students have the longest and most demanding program. It involves five to nine years of study, depending on whether a student wishes to be a family doctor, a specialist in a particular field of medicine, a medical researcher, or a teacher of other doctors.

The first four years are spent in medical school learning the fundamentals. The students shown below, for example, devoted every morning for three months to dissecting human corpses, or cadavers, to learn how the body is constructed and how it functions.

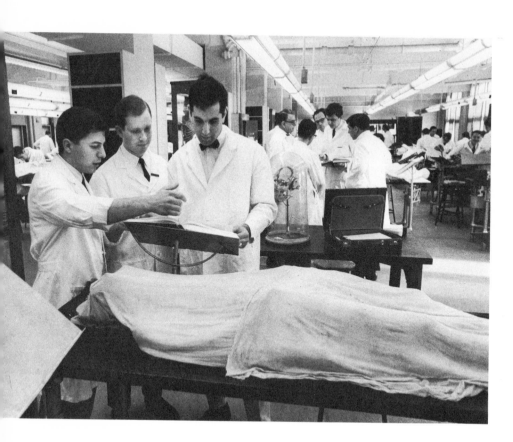

These students are accompanying a physician on his rounds in one of the university's teaching hospitals. The girls in gray blouses are student nurses.

When a student receives his medical degree he joins the staff of a hospital where, depending on his goals, he spends from one to five years more in training. Ordinarily he is not ready to start his career until he is in his late twenties or early thirties. However, for many young people the long period of preparation is not a deterrent. Each year the medical school receives 2,000 applications for the 130 places available in its entering class.

Dental students at this university are trained to serve two roles. One is the familiar role of the specialist who cares for the teeth and gums. They also are prepared to serve as troubleshooters who advise patients on health problems that may be developing elsewhere in the body. It is a logical role since a dentist sees his patients more regularly than a doctor, and it is in the mouth that the first sign of a disease frequently appears. This might be only a slight change in the color of the gums, but to the trained eye of the dentist it could suggest something amiss that should be checked by a doctor.

Students in the dental school spend their third and fourth years working in the clinic shown above. There are 133 treatment stations in this vast room. Each student is assigned ten patients who pay the university a small fee for the care they receive. Their student dentist

94

works with them regularly in much the same way that a full-fledged dentist conducts his practice. An important difference for the patient is that here he actually has two dentists—the student and a faculty member who closely supervises what is done.

In the photograph on this page the patient is a calf with a broken left front leg and its doctor is a fourth year student in the School of Veterinary Medicine. The calf is being treated at the university's animal hospital in an agricultural area thirty miles from the campus. Here students care for cattle, sheep, goats, and horses that are sick or disabled. They also make frequent trips to nearby farms to see patients not sick enough to be hospitalized. In addition, they serve in the animal clinic on the main campus where they learn to care for dogs, cats, and other pets.

When a student graduates he is prepared to treat over fifty different species of animals, many of which suffer from diseases peculiar to their species. He also has a knowledge of more than one hundred diseases that animals pass on to man. As a result, he knows almost as much about human medicine as he does about animal medicine.

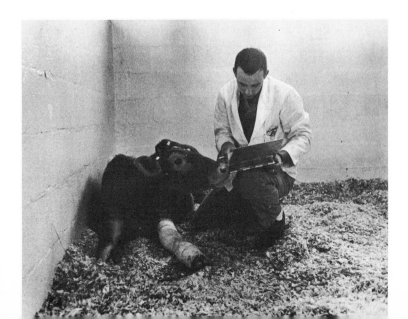

The law students shown on the next page are arguing a case in a practice, or moot, court. At such hearings
the students do not represent real clients. However, the
opposing arguments they present are based on hours
of research and thought and the judges frequently are
important men who have volunteered their time to hear
the students. In fact, the judge at the center of the

photograph on page 96 is William J. Brennan of the United States Supreme Court.

The arguments at this hearing concerned the right of an individual to conduct a civil rights demonstration in a restaurant or some other private building used by the public. Whenever necessary the judges interrupted to challenge a student's facts, reasoning, or conclusions.

At the end of the hearing they decided which student had presented the best case.

Arguing cases in a courtroom is, of course, but one aspect of a lawyer's work. He serves his clients as an advisor on legal matters and may represent them in their dealings with others, serving as a negotiator or a peacemaker. Still other lawyers hold positions in government where they deal not only with legal matters but with the problems that confront society.

The training this law school offers is, as a result, very broad. In the three years a student attends he studies not only the law but such subjects as economics, urban life, international affairs, and psychology, and how these subjects relate to the law.

He also has an opportunity to obtain practical experience. Some students, for example, help attorneys operate neighborhood law offices which assist poor people with legal problems. Others help men and women in prison obtain legal advice. In addition, a number teach weekly classes in the local high schools to help

young people learn to see the law as an ally, not an enemy.

In addition to this university's 14,000 full-time students, there are 4,000 who attend part time. Most work at jobs or have families to care for and attend classes in the evenings or on Saturdays. Some have a bachelor's degree as a goal, which under these circumstances requires at least eight years and great persistence. Others are working toward an advanced degree. But many more take only a course or two now and then. All they wish as a reward is to learn.

The Faculty

Not too many years ago teaching at a university was a peaceful but poorly paid job. Relatively little research was undertaken, a limited number of graduate students were trained, and few professors were actively involved with the problems of the world. The emphasis was on teaching undergraduates.

Things have changed. When I asked a professor at the university to describe his job, he groaned. "It is so complicated," he said, "my head reels." Each semester he teaches a course for undergraduates, helps train a number of graduate students, and does research. In addition he is a member of a faculty committee concerned with undergraduate affairs and three other committees that deal with the operation of his department.

He is also faculty advisor to a group of freshmen and

is available several hours a week to other students who want to see him. Periodically he leaves the university to teach for a year at another school as a visiting professor. Moreover, he writes articles and books, attends conferences throughout the world on his field of interest, and serves as a paid consultant to two government agencies.

At this university there are 1,600 faculty members with similar schedules.* Most spend from a third to half of their time teaching. The rest is devoted to research and to administrative work on the many committees that help operate the university. As the responsibilities of the faculty have increased, so have their salaries, which now range from about $7,000 a year to $25,000.

Traditionally, a faculty member served at one or two universities during his entire career. This also has changed. Many professors today feel a stronger loyalty to their field of study than they do to a university. Moreover, other schools do not hesitate to entice them away with better opportunities for advancement and research. As a result, every year at least one faculty member in ten leaves this university for another.

There are, in a sense, two faculties here. There is a junior faculty that consists of young instructors and assistant professors who lack experience but have their Ph.D., which has become a basic requirement for teaching in a university. There also is a senior faculty which consists largely of associate professors and full professors who not only have experience but tenure.

A professor with tenure cannot be fired. As a result, he is free to teach his courses in the way he wishes, express opinions that may be unpopular with officials

* There also are 2,800 men and women who teach part time while holding full-time jobs in other professions.

102

of the university and others, and undertake whatever research he chooses. Moreover, if he moves to another school he often takes his tenure with him.

A faculty member ordinarily is granted tenure after seven years of teaching if he has demonstrated his ability as a teacher and a research scholar. However, it often is difficult to determine how effective a teacher is. In many fields a man's classroom is literally his castle and may not be visited by other teachers or by university officials. In such cases his superiors must rely to a considerable extent on his reputation with students.

Reaching conclusions about his research is easier. Most faculty members are regularly expected to conduct original research which contributes to man's knowledge, then report on what they have learned by writing articles and books. Faculty members without tenure are likely to lose their jobs if they do not undertake research. As they describe it, they must "publish or perish."

On the other hand, artists, architects, composers, musicians, and writers who teach are not expected to do research. They are judged on the basis of the painting, sculpture, or buildings they create or the novels or musical compositions they write or the performances they give in concerts.

At this university about half the beginning teachers eventually are granted tenure. The others either move on to another university or college where they try again or they enter another profession.

As officials of this university see it, the most effective teachers are those who are deeply involved in projects on the frontiers of knowledge. However, not everyone agrees. Some educators maintain that a man may be an excellent teacher without doing any research. They also complain that some faculty members are far more interested in research than in teaching and as a result do not spend enough time with their students.

The amount of research at the universities in this country has increased in an extraordinary way since the 1950s. It was in that period that the Federal government began paying the cost of large-scale research projects to help strengthen the nation in its "cold war" with the Soviet Union. The objectives were to expand our knowledge in the sciences and to train scientists and other specialists of the future. Soon foundations and business firms were contributing large sums to support research that interested them. In the process, this university and others became major research centers.

In a recent year, the faculty members here, with the help of their graduate students, were involved in over nine hundred research projects in almost every conceivable field. Their work concerned such varied matters as egg formation in the moth, decision making in American cities, the prevention of cancer, and the development of mini-cars.

In many cases, as has been noted, the research was concerned with solving a particular problem; in others the objective was the traditional one at universities: replacing ignorance with knowledge and thereby broadening our understanding of the world. A number of these projects required millions of dollars, elaborate equipment, and teams of faculty members, research associates, graduate students, and technicians.* Others involved but a few thousand dollars, a single faculty member, and only one or two graduate students.

* A research associate is a full-time researcher on the university staff, but not a faculty member.

That year the faculty received thirty-nine million dollars for research. Of this amount five million came from foundations and business firms and the rest from agencies of the Federal government, including the Department of Defense, the Atomic Energy Commission, the Public Health Service, the National Science Foundation, and the Office of Education. Throughout the country that year universities spent more than one and a half billion dollars on research.

Just what does a research project involve? Let's consider several with different objectives and different approaches.

Each of the millions of cells that make up the human body consists of a microscopic quantity of protoplasm and a nucleus. Inside the nucleus are forty-six rodlike objects called chromosomes that provide the "instructions" a cell needs to function normally.

For the body to develop and to repair itself a cell must be able to create new cells. Before one cell can create another, however, each of its chromosomes must create a new chromosome. The chromosomes then separate into two groups which, in turn, separate into identical cells. The process by which this is done is called mitosis.

There are still many unanswered questions regarding mitosis. One of the most important concerns the ability of the chromosomes to move from one position to another in a cell and rearrange themselves in separate groups. Just how they move is a puzzle that a biologist at the university, Dr. Hidemi Sato, is attempting to solve.

In his research he is studying the behavior of chromosomes in the relatively large, easily observed cells of

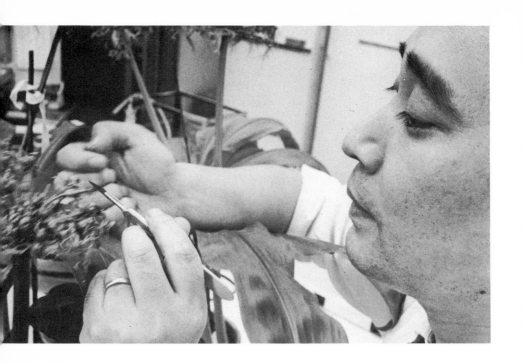

the African lily. In the photograph above he is removing a seed pod from a lily plant.

He then cuts into the pod, places a drop of its endosperm fluid on a slide, and studies the cell he finds, using high-powered microscopes and cameras to do so.

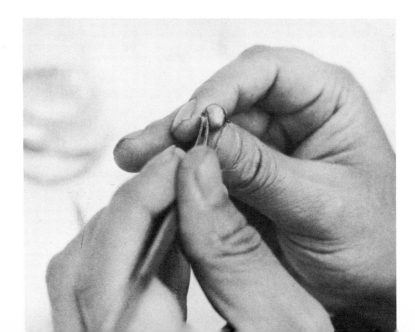

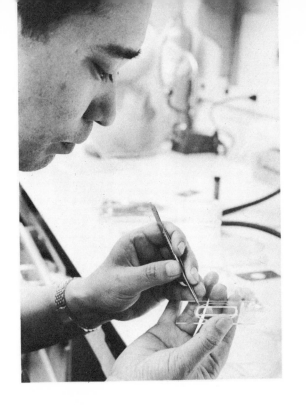

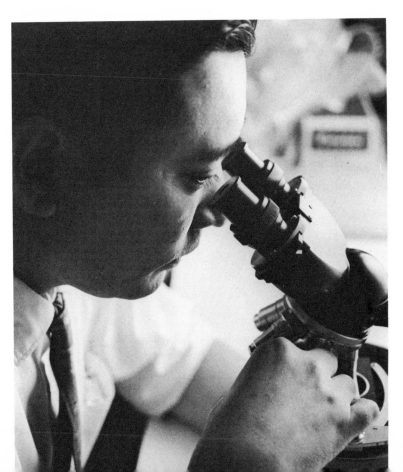

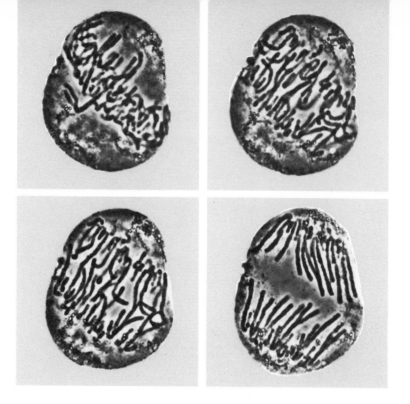

These photographs of a lily cell, taken at intervals, show the movement of the chromosomes as the cell prepares to separate.* About an hour is needed for the chromosomes to move into position. The photographs were taken during a twenty-seven-minute period toward the end of this cycle.

It already has been found that clusters of fibers extending from the center of a chromosome pull it from one position to another. In the photograph at the lower right the fibers are at the base of the V each chromosome has formed. It also has been found that chromosomes are pulled at the same rate of speed no matter how large or small they are. Why this is so is not known. Just how the fibers operate also is not known.

The answers to such questions will provide a clearer

* The actual diameter of this cell is equal to that of a human hair. Here it is magnified about five hundred times.

understanding of mitosis. They will also bring us some-what closer to an understanding of how cancer occurs, a disease in which cells ignore their "instructions" and grow out of control. However, before we can determine what has gone wrong in a cancerous cell, we must first understand what normal behavior is and how it occurs.

During the first half of the seventh century a merchant ship with a cargo of a thousand wine jars sank in 120 feet of water after hitting a reef near Yassi Ada, or Yassi Island, off what today is the west coast of Turkey. It was one of dozens of ships that over the centuries have gone down in these treacherous waters.

When a team of underwater archaeologists from this university began to explore the graveyard 1,300 years later, it was the wine carrier to which they turned first.

Over a period of three summers they brought to the surface the remaining fragments of its deck, ribs, and hull, as well as wine jars, tools, tableware, lamps, coins, and a balance for weighing cargo that carried the inscription *George, Senior Sea Captain.*

Many of the coins they found were like the one shown above, carrying the image and the name of Heraclius, who ruled the Byzantine Empire at the eastern end of the Mediterranean Sea from 610 to 641. From such evidence the archaeologists were able to determine how old the ship was and identify it as Byzantine. Moreover, once they had learned these facts, they could assume that everything aboard dated from this period.

Because of advances in diving equipment, thousands of ancient wrecks untouched for centuries now are within reach of archaeologists and historians. As these ships are excavated our knowledge of daily life in the distant past steadily increases. So does what we know of trade, migration, and ship construction.

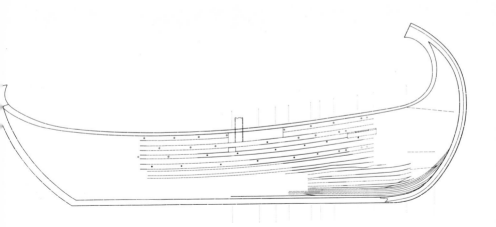

One of the fascinating discoveries regarding the Byzantine wreck involved the ship itself. Although little remained, painstaking measurement enabled the archaeologists to create a detailed plan of the sixty-five-foot vessel. It turned out to be the earliest known craft in which planks were nailed to a frame of ribs, a method still used in building wooden ships. Of course, whether an archaeologist works under water or on land, his objectives are the same: to excavate, preserve, and interpret the remains of earlier civilizations and thereby provide man with a better understanding of his past. But the methods used by an underwater archaeologist are quite different from those used by his colleagues on land.

An expedition on land may involve one or two archaeologists and a crew of laborers who handle whatever digging is necessary. An underwater expedition relies on a great many trained specialists, from oceanographers to engineers, mechanics, and boatmen. The archaeologists themselves are not only scholars but

skilled divers who often must work at great depths in chill water, dim light, and strong currents. The time they can spend below, moreover, is often limited to less than an hour a day because of the ever-present threat of the dread disease called bends.*

The underwater archaeologists at the university also rely on elaborate equipment. In searching for wrecks, for example, they make use of sonar and a two-man submarine. The oceanographer shown above is checking a sonar record aboard a search vessel to determine if high frequency vibrations scanning the sea bed have

* If a diver remains below too long and ascends to the surface too rapidly nitrogen in the body forms bubbles in the blood stream or the spinal fluid. This, in turn, may result in crippling or death.

detected anything. When they do the submarine is dispatched to investigate.

In excavating a wreck the archaeologists work from a barge. First, they dive to the sea bed with probes and metal detectors to determine how much of the remains are covered with sand. Next, they erect a scaffold of angle irons over the wreck to guide them in plotting its size and recording the position of each object they find. They use a variety of techniques to remove the sand that may cover a wreck. The large pipe seen above is an airlift which sucks up loose sand. The fire hose the diver is holding is used to dislodge more stubborn material. With fragile objects a diver removes the sand a handful at a time.

When all the objects on the sea bed have been exposed, they are tagged to indicate their precise location. The site is then "mapped" with photographs taken with cameras and lights attached to the submarine. The photograph below was made at 130 feet. It shows part of the hull of a Roman wreck at least 200 years older than the Byzantine ship.

After the photographs are made, everything that can be moved is taken ashore. Small objects are packed in baskets and carried to the surface by lifting balloons. Large pieces, such as a ship's timbers, are placed in still larger baskets which are "walked up" the slope of the sea's floor to the nearest beach. When the sea bed is finally cleared, the archaeologists probe deeper into the sand in search of other remains.

Meanwhile the objects that have been removed are cleaned, photographed, catalogued, and studied. As the work progresses, the story of an ancient ship slowly takes shape.

At the university's Center for Studies in Criminology there are a hundred charts like the one on the next page. Together they provide a picture of who the juvenile delinquents in this country are, the kind and number of offenses they commit, and the ages at which they do so.

The charts are based on information gathered in a five-year study of ten thousand boys between the ages of ten and eighteen. On the basis of what they have learned the researchers hope to predict which types of juvenile delinquents are likely to commit a second offense, how serious it might be, and how much time might elapse before it is likely to occur. Such information would be of great value to police and to the courts in suggesting which boys might be headed for trouble.

The research was carried out in the city where the university has its campus. By checking school records, information was obtained on each boy's IQ, school achievement, school attendance, family income, and race, as well as on the kinds of neighborhoods in which he had lived over the years.

The researchers then checked local police records to learn which boys had committed offenses, how many they had committed, how serious they were, and how old the boys were on each occasion.

With the help of a computer they next tried to find patterns of delinquency—whether certain offenses were committed at certain ages; whether boys whose first offense occurred early had more serious offenses later; whether IQ, race, family income, and other factors were related to certain kinds of delinquency. Using the patterns they found, the researchers then attempted to determine what the chances were that boys with certain characteristics would behave in certain ways.

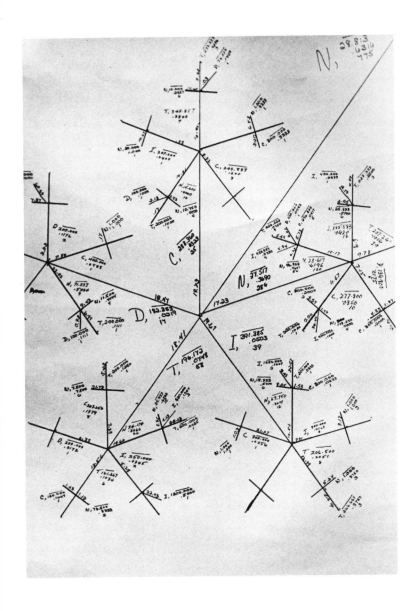

The chart above illustrates a portion of what was learned about boys from families with incomes of $100 a week. Of the 3,000 boys in this group, the researchers found that 1,100 had committed at least one offense, usually by the time they were 14. With 775 of them, the offense was minor, such as skipping school or loitering on a street corner. The rest were involved in more serious crimes such as stealing or injuring someone. The researchers then grouped the boys by the types of offenses they had committed, and determined what had happened to each group in the years that followed.

Our chart follows the careers of the 775 boys whose first offense was a minor one. It shows that 425 went on to commit a second offense, usually 17 to 19 months later. Two hundred and eighty-six of these offenses were also minor. They are represented on the chart by the symbol N_1. But the rest involved thefts (T_1), injury to another person (I_1), property damage (D_1), and a combination of two or more such crimes (C_1). The chart also shows how many boys in each of these categories went on to commit still other offenses.

Of course, the 775 boys represented here also are represented in dozens of other charts which analyze delinquency in terms of IQ, school attendance, and other factors. This is also the case with the thousands of other boys in this study. When all this information is brought together and analyzed, the researchers hope to have their answers.

Although this research was still under way when this book was written, the researchers already had found it possible to draw some general conclusions. The most interesting was that one boy in three in the population may commit an offense that involves the police and that half of these boys are likely to commit a second offense.

Nuclear physicists at this university are probing deep into the heart of the atom. Their laboratory is a ten-

million-dollar research center which the university and another nearby operate jointly for the Atomic Energy Commission.

The task, as one physicist explained it, is opening "boxes," then trying to understand the complex behavior of the particles found inside. The largest one of these "boxes" is, of course, the atom, yet it is extraordinarily small. An ordinary cube of sugar, for example, might contain as many as 10,000,000,000,000,000,000,000,000 individual atoms.

Inside each atom there are one or more electrons and a nucleus. Inside each nucleus there are tiny particles known as protons and neutrons. When these particles are broken apart they yield still other particles known as mesons. Whether there are smaller, more basic particles is not yet known.

Breaking into the nucleus to study its particles requires enormous force. To generate the energy needed, the physicists at this university rely on a three billion electron volt accelerator or "atom smasher," one of the world's most powerful. The control room is shown on the preceding page. The accelerator itself with its magnets, voltage generators, and other high-powered electrical equipment is contained in a huge, doughnut-shaped concrete structure one hundred feet across and thirty feet high.

Think of the accelerator as a gun that fires bullets with such force that they are able to penetrate the nucleus of the atom and break apart the particles it contains. The "bullets" are protons taken from the atoms that make up hydrogen gas. Each hydrogen atom consists of a single electron and a nucleus. Unlike other atoms, however, its nucleus contains but one proton and no neutrons.

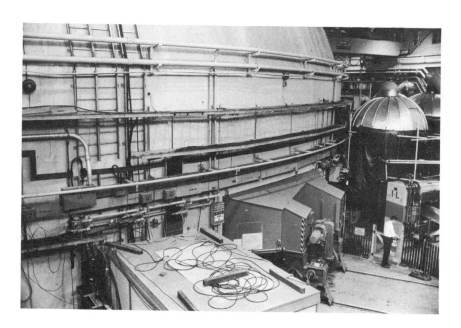

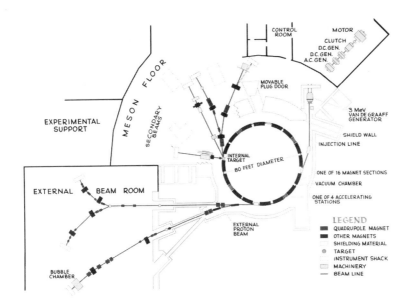

The gas is placed in a Van de Graaff generator. The location is shown in the diagram above. It then is subjected to an electrical charge which strips the electron from each of the atoms. All that remains are the protons. These are fed into an airless circular tunnel two and three-quarter inches high, eleven inches wide, and 240 feet long. When the tunnel is filled it contains 50,000 million protons.

The protons then are formed into a beam about a quarter of an inch in circumference which is pushed rapidly through the tunnel by an electric field the generators create. As the beam moves around and around, guided by magnets, its velocity builds to 180,000 miles per second, almost the speed of light. As the speed of the protons increases, so does the amount of energy they contain.

In but a fortieth of a second the proton beam makes 100,000 trips through the tunnel, a distance of over

121

4,000 miles. Then it is hurled at its target, which might be a small piece of copper, platinum, or carbon, or some other substance that is useful to the researchers. When the protons strike the target they penetrate tens of thousands of atoms, freeing the particles the physicists need for their research. A new beam is released twenty times a second.

This is one of the research areas adjoining the accelerator. Here and elsewhere in the building a dozen teams of researchers are at work. The beam of protons is channeled to their apparatus through concrete tunnels. Since the beam and the particles it frees are radioactive, many precautions are taken to protect researchers and other workers against exposure. Huge blocks of iron and concrete serve as radiation shields. Badges which record exposure to radiation must be worn by everyone. And signs like those on page 123 are everywhere.

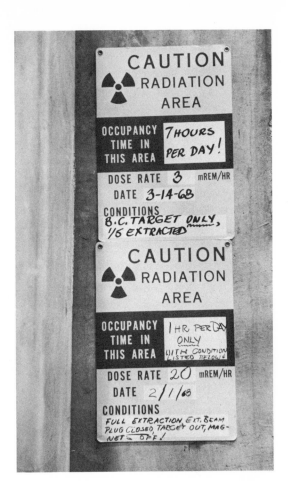

In a far corner of this room a team of six physicists and three graduate students from the university are concentrating their research on the behavior of the K meson or kaon, one of the many types of mesons that emerge from the proton and the neutron. However, almost as soon as the kaon appears—usually within .00000012 of a second—it disintegrates into other kinds of particles.

How does one study what he cannot see, particularly if it exists for almost no time at all? For their observa-

tions the scientists in this group use the spark chamber shown above which consists of a series of giant electric plates immersed in a mixture of helium and neon gases.

When a beam of protons frees particles from a nearby target, those needed for the research are automatically sorted out and focused into a new beam which collides with still another target. The particles resulting from this second collision fly through the spark chamber. Since they are electrically charged they interact with the gas, leaving in their wake tracks of

124

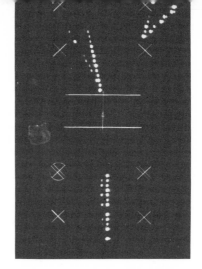

sparks which are automatically photographed. Hundreds of thousands of photographs like this one might be made during the course of a single experiment.

Meanwhile elaborate electronic recording equipment measures the behavior of the kaons. The scientists are trying to learn whether they behave in predictable ways. They are concerned, for example, with the angles at which they move, the momentum they achieve, the kinds of particles into which they decay, and how these particles affect still others. Patterns are emerging, but as in all research no one knows precisely where the trail will lead.

The final step in a research project is the preparation of a report which summarizes the findings and their significance for other scientists or scholars. Most such reports appear as articles in one or another of the 95,000 learned journals published throughout the world. In the sciences alone, over 100,000 such articles are published each year.

Longer research reports may appear as books. About 3,000 are issued each year by the universities themselves. They do so through nonprofit publishing departments called "university presses." There are about eighty such presses throughout the country, including the one operated by this university.

Their objective is to publish important scholarly books which otherwise might not appear because they have such limited audiences and offer a commerical publisher little chance for making a profit. An example of such a book is *The Selected Guide to the Literature on the Flowering Plants of Mexico*, which this university published for the few botanists concerned with that region. It sold only 350 copies, yet met a serious need. The university press here issues, in all, about 25 new books a year, some of which are shown on the preceding page.

When a report on a research project is published, it is then evaluated by other experts whose opinions appear in reviews in the learned journals. At times they praise a report for its contribution, but not always.

A research report frequently consists of more than a book or an article. In the case of archaeologists, anthropologists, or botanists, for example, it may also include many objects or specimens gathered during the research. At this university the most interesting of these are displayed in the university museum or in smaller departmental museums where students and the public can see them and visiting scholars can use them in any research they are conducting.

There also are a number of faculty members who do not conduct research. They include, as noted earlier, artists, musicians, writers, and others who combine teaching with careers in their creative fields.

The man shown above, for example, is George Crumb, an associate professor of music who is also a composer. When this photograph was taken in his studio at the university he was setting to music the poems of Federico García Lorca, a young poet and dramatist who was killed during the Spanish Civil War.

Dr. Crumb is a composer of the so-called "new music" in which the major and minor keys, basic to traditional music, are not used. The result, he feels, is a freer kind of music which offers many more possibilities for expression. In "Echoes of Time and the River,"

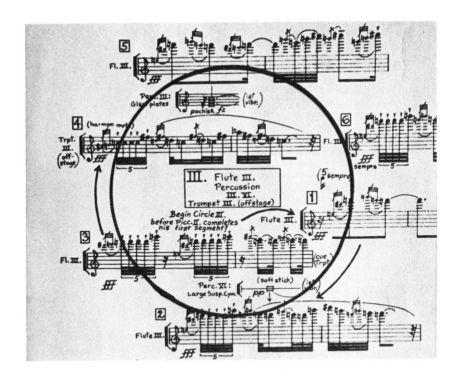

a symphony for which he was awarded a Pulitzer Prize, he used a great many unusual approaches to create the effects he wanted.

The brass and wind musicians, for example, play into the piano strings to create "sympathetic vibrations." The pianists play their instruments with their knuckles or palms or with wooden mallets. One player beats on a gong as he lowers it into a tub containing nine inches of water. Other musicians march about as they play.

"Echoes" also includes sections that Dr. Crumb calls "circle music" in which musicians are given an opportunity to play at their own pace rather than at one prescribed by the composer. The score for such an interlude is reproduced above.

When this work first was played by the Chicago

Symphony Orchestra it drew enthusiastic cheers from many of the audience, although others felt the music was disorganized and discordant and booed vigorously.

As with most composers, Dr. Crumb's objective is to express through his music a mood or an idea. He first imagines the effects he wants, then works out in his mind and on paper the combination of sounds needed to achieve them. He may rework a passage a dozen times until it seems right. Occasionally he will test a sound on a piano, but far more often he simply listens to an imagined sound. In fact, it is not until his work is first played in rehearsal by an orchestra that he actually hears what he has created.

As we have seen, a good deal of the work of the faculty takes place in the quiet isolation of a laboratory, a library, an office, or a studio. But a growing number also have become involved with the world beyond the campus. Hundreds of faculty members at this university now grapple with the problems of urban renewal, housing, air pollution, poverty, unemployment, civil rights, education, labor relations, and other matters of deep concern.

In some cases they do so as advisors to governments, companies, action groups, and other organizations that deal with such problems. But many also conduct research and training programs that directly affect the lives and the fortunes of people here and abroad.

This university sprawls along the edge of what was once a fine neighborhod, but today is a decaying ghetto called Mantua. The semester I visited the campus the leaders in Mantua had turned to the university for help. They were planning programs to improve housing,

health, education, and job opportunities and needed assistance in training people from the community to run them.

The university's Human Resources Program made the arrangements. Using faculty members and other experts, it trained a half-dozen young men and women for these jobs. In turn, they trained the others needed, using faculty members as advisors. The photograph above shows one of these sessions.

The project is but one of many the Human Resources Program has carried out in Mantua and other ghettos in the city. Its objectives are to improve conditions in these areas and in the process learn more about dealing with the problems of ghetto life. As a result, its activities have covered a broad range: from

131

teaching illiterate adults to read and write, to helping high school dropouts make a good life for themselves. In the latter case, the Human Resources Program asked a hundred local boys who had dropped out of high school for their help in planning and testing such an effort.

For six weeks one summer the boys lived in dormitories at the university. In the mornings they attended classes. The rest of the day they worked at jobs either at the university or in the ghettos. Those shown above, for example, built a neighborhood play lot. The evenings were devoted to cultural activities and recreation.

132

In a study three months later, the boys reported that their goals were far higher as a result of the experience, and so were their hopes for the future.

A team of economists at the university have a professional interest in the future. Every three months they issue a forecast they have made as to how prosperous the nation will be during the months ahead.

What they conclude is highly useful to businessmen in planning their economic strategy. For example, it may help manufacturers estimate the sales they can expect and determine what their production schedule should be. It also may help them decide whether to increase their work force, purchase new equipment, or go ahead with construction of a new plant.

The forecast is derived from a series of 76 equations which represent 118 factors that determine how prosperous the country is. When the equations are solved they provide a prediction of the wages that will be paid, the amount of unemployment there will be, the amount of construction that will take place, the cost of borrowing money, and dozens of other highly important conditions.

This equation, for example, predicts what the sale of cars and automobile parts will be.

$$C_a = 48.54 + \underset{(0.0228)}{0.1346} \left(Y - \frac{T_r}{p_c} \right) - \underset{(10.20)}{54.19} \frac{p_a}{p_c}$$

$$- \underset{(0.175)}{0.430}\, Un - \underset{(0.458)}{4.129}\, \delta_s + \underset{(0.478)}{1.835}\, Cr - \underset{(0.0180)}{0.0744}\, K_{a_{-1}}$$

It takes into account how much income people currently have (represented by Y in the equation), how much unemployment there is (Un), and the existing

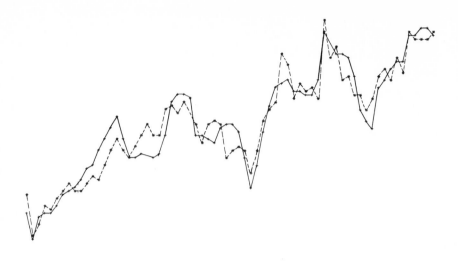

stock of automobiles (K_a). It also relies on other facts
which are obtained when some of the other equations
are solved.

When the economists have gathered the information
they need for their forecast, it is fed into a computer.
Within seconds they have a picture of what the future
will hold. As the graph above shows, and businessmen
have come to recognize, the forecast is remarkably accurate. The solid line stands for car sales over a sixteen-
year period. The broken line represents what the economists predicted they would be.

The Law School's Prison Research Council deals with
information of a different kind. The letter on the next
page was written by an inmate at a state prison nearby.
It is one of hundreds the Council receives each year
from prisoners who want help with legal problems.

Most believe they were dealt with unfairly in their
trials and ask for advice on what to do. The professors

134

and the law students who make up the staff of the Council answer every question they receive. Where necessary, they check the law, review the records and testimony in a case, and even interview the policemen and lawyers involved.

Once or twice a year there is a happy ending. A complaint seems justified, a lawyer volunteers to represent the prisoner, and the prisoner is either set free or has his sentence reduced.

Dear Sir,

I am an inmate of the State Correctional Institution at Huntingdon, Pennsylvania,

On Thursday morning February 23/67 while listening to the radio it was said that your school may be able to give assistance to an inmate if it were shown that he may have sound grounds on which to build a case.

Sir I believe that I have the right grounds but lack the knowledge to go about it the right way. I have been going on what the so-called jailhouse lawyer said, as I have no other means or way of finding out how to go about these things.

I hope that your school can help me, and I thank you for any time this letter take up.

Very sincerely Yours

University programs also have affected the lives of farmers in India and students in Iran. The Indian project involved the Peace Corps. Faculty members and others at the university trained sixty-one young men and women to help farmers in the State of Gujarat improve their food production. The Corpsmen were trained a hundred miles from the main campus at a mountain retreat the university turned into an Indian village.

It included a bazaar of shops and a restaurant staffed by Indians, the small tin-roofed Hindu temple shown in the photograph where Corpsmen learned Indian religious customs, several acres where Indian crops were grown, a small rice paddy, and large numbers of goats and chickens which ran free, as they would have done in India. Moreover, Indian rupees were used as currency and only Gujarati was spoken.

In Iran the project involved Pahlavi University, a new school in Shiraz which members of the faculty and staff at this university helped establish. They provided advice on organizing the school, prepared a ninety-page manual on how to run it, and trained Iranians to serve on its faculty and staff. They also continue to help whenever new problems arise.

Along with the official faculty there are a dozen chaplains on this campus who are teachers of a different kind. They conduct religious services and offer advice on personal problems, but they also serve in other roles.

A number are deeply involved in social action. They demonstrate against war and the draft, work in behalf of those in the ghettos, and speak their minds freely whenever there is a need to be heard. During disagreements between student groups and the university, chaplains also have intervened to bring the two sides together. In addition, some serve the university as a persistent conscience, raising questions about the wisdom and the ethics of decisions that strike them as unwise or unfair.

When they see a problem the university does nothing to solve they may try to find solutions on their own. As one result, they established a service which gives students information and advice on conscientious ob-

jection and other matters relating to the draft. The
Episcopal chaplain in the photograph is counseling a
student who within a year faces military service.

The chaplains also established the Catacombs, the
student coffeehouse described earlier. Formerly, students had no place on campus where they could spend
an evening drinking coffee and listening to music. Now
the Catacombs is jammed every night it is open.

There also are other teachers here—a steady stream
of poets, politicians, publishers, and journalists—who

for a fee address student groups and later perhaps meet with them informally. One of these was the poet Allen Ginsberg. In the photograph below he is taking tea with a group of students at the Dirty Drug.

The Administration

A great many years ago the faculty handled all the details involved in running the universities where they taught. Of course, as the schools grew larger and more complicated, this became impractical, and gradually other persons took over these duties. Today almost as many people are needed to operate a university as are needed to teach the students and carry on research.

In all, more than 600 officials are needed to manage the affairs of this university. They range from a president, his various assistants, and numerous deans to experts in finance, fund-raising, and publicity. Together they make up what is known as the administration. To help these officials the university also employs 3,000 secretaries, clerks, and other workers.

The administration is headed by a Board of Trustees which is legally responsible for the welfare of the uni-

141

versity. Its forty members are leading citizens and in most cases also alumni of the school. The Board assembles three times a year to review the condition of the university and make major policy decisions. It is shown at one of these meetings in the photograph on page 140. In addition, small committees of the trustees meet each month with university officials to make decisions on finances, faculty appointments, and other matters.

Ten of the trustees are elected by the alumni. The rest are named by the Board itself to replace members who retire or resign. Some trustees are selected in honor of their distinguished careers or their long service to the university. Others are chosen because of special skills, such as a background in law or finance, or because of a link they provide to government leaders or other key groups.

Frequently a person's wealth also is a factor in his selection. In such cases there is a hope that he may contribute large sums to the university, which at times is just what happens. In a recent fund-raising campaign, for example, the trustees together gave the school sixteen million dollars.

The man in the photograph is the president of this university. Once he was chairman of the Physics Department, but in those days life was less complicated. His job now is to make the university work effectively. To do this he must be sure that the eighteen schools and colleges here, the many academic departments, the thousands of faculty members, and the hundreds of administrators work together to meet the university's objectives.

He also must be certain that the needs of students,

142

faculty, and alumni are being met. In addition, he must take into account relationships with the world beyond the campus, particularly with the city where the university is located, with the state which each year contributes several million dollars to balance the budget, and with Federal agencies whose financial support also is needed.

The president also oversees a vast building program, encourages wealthy alumni to give money, and participates in countless meetings and special events. In addition, each year he teaches an undergraduate course in physics.

There are a great many officials who help the president with his job. These include a provost who has responsibility for academic affairs, vice-provosts in charge of student affairs and research, and vice-presidents in charge of fund-raising and government relations. Each of these has dozens of people working for him.

There are planners such as the men shown above who help carry out expansion of the university, financial experts who deal with the problems of the budget, fund raisers who try to raise the money needed, and alumni secretaries who keep the 125,000 alumni informed about the school.

There also is a team of public relations men who advise university officials on policies relating to the public, prepare a dozen magazines and newsletters, produce TV programs and motion pictures, and help writers develop articles and also books such as this one.

There also are employment specialists who help find jobs for students about to graduate, such as the student above who is being interviewed by a visiting employer. There is a buildings and grounds department staffed by engineers, architects, and draftsmen; there is a health service, a faculty club, dining rooms, a book store, a printing plant, a purchasing department, and a police force.

145

In addition to their duties as teachers and researchers, faculty members here have a strong voice in determining the policies that govern the university. This is the case at many schools, but not at every one.

At this university the faculty elects thirty-nine representatives to a body called the University Council. There they work with the president and other officials in developing approaches to admissions policies, student discipline, community relations, and other problems that confront the university. Much of the Council's work is conducted through committees, one of which is shown above. The committees concerned with student life, as we have seen, also have student members.

The operation of individual schools and academic departments also is the responsibility of the faculty. This, too, is handled by committees on which they serve.

The president of this university says his biggest problem is finding all the money needed to operate the school. It is a problem that plagues almost every university and college in the country. Even publicly-owned schools such as state universities are not immune.

At the root of the problem are the rapidly increasing number of students, the ever-growing need for new buildings, and the rising salaries faculty members command.

The problem is even more difficult for universities than for colleges. One reason is that universities have a large and growing number of graduate students. Educating them costs at least three times as much as educating undergraduates. Another reason is the extent to which universities rely on the Federal government for financial help. In research projects, as an example, the government not only pays for the research but often pays the salaries of faculty members involved and the tuition and living expenses of the graduate students who help them.

The University's Expenses	
Instruction and related activities	46 %
Research	26 %
Administration, miscellaneous	15 %
Student financial aid	8 %
Maintenance of the campus	3 %
Libraries	2 %

The University's Income

Income from hospitals, dining services	30 %
Funds from Federal government	29 %
Student tuition and fees	22 %
Funds from state government	8 %
Gifts and grants	7 %
Invested funds (endowment)	4 %

At this university the Federal contribution for research, scholarships, and construction has amounted to almost 40 million dollars a year. When the Congress decides to reduce such expenditures, as it does in some years, the university either must find money to make up for the reduction or cut back on its programs.

The year this book was written the university spent 120 million dollars on its operations, compared with 40 million dollars ten years earlier. The chart on the preceding page shows how the money was spent. The chart above shows where it came from.

As the chart above indicates, the university received almost 60 per cent of its income from the Federal government and from its hospitals and dining services. In each case, though, income barely covered expenses.

On the other hand, the tuition students pay comes nowhere near meeting the cost of their education. Even though tuition continues to rise, it barely covers the salaries of the faculty. The rest of what is needed must come from three other sources: endowment, gifts, and as noted earlier, the state government.

A university's endowment consists of contributions it has received over the years which have been invested in stocks and bonds and earn income in the form of dividends and interest. This university has one of the largest endowments in the country. It amounts to 165 million dollars and earns close to 5 million dollars a year which is used to meet current expenses.

In a recent year the university also received 38,000 individual contributions which came to 21 million dollars. Some of this was added to the endowment, but most was spent for day-to-day operations and for research. The gifts came from alumni, from people who had not attended the school but wished to support it anyway, and from companies and foundations. Throughout the country that year universities and colleges received one and a half billion dollars in gifts.

A few such contributions are enormous. When this photograph was taken it had just been announced that the man walking at the left had given the university a half million dollars for a new cultural center.

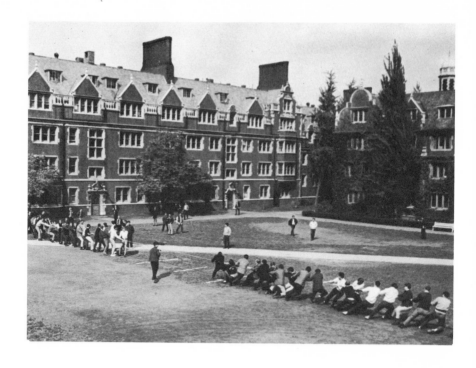

An End
and a Beginning

Hey Day is the traditional climax to the school year at this university. It is then that the classes formally move up. Freshmen become sophomores, sophomores become juniors, and juniors at long last become seniors. There still are examinations to take which could change things somewhat, but on this day at least no one seems concerned.

Early in the afternoon the freshmen and the sophomores test their strength in a tug of war. The freshmen, at the left in the photograph, won easily.

Sporting straw hats and canes, the juniors then assemble on the steps of the men's quadrangle. They sing the "Red and Blue" and other songs, then march across the campus to Irvine Auditorium where the year's awards for scholarship and leadership are to be made.

Among the highest awards are those that go to the

151

four senior honor men who receive, as is traditional, a cane, a spoon, a bowl, and a spade. The ceremonies also involve a fragile silk academic gown which has been passed from the outgoing senior class to the incoming senior class each year since 1887.

When the ceremonies are over, the honor men plant a sprig of ivy to leave their mark for future generations of students.

For most of the 18,000 students here the school year ends with final examinations. When these are over they pack their belongings and return home to await the results. Of course, for seniors and for advanced students who have finished their work commencement lies ahead.

The Saturday and Sunday before commencement is Alumni Weekend. Over two thousand men and women who graduated in previous years return to the campus with their families to see old friends and relive their college days. There are parties, tours, entertainment, meetings, and a series of lectures by faculty members.

The final event is a parade of the alumni and their families, led by the oldest graduating class present. In this case it was the Class of 1898, which was represented by one of its few surviving members. When there are a large number of alumni from a class they often parade in costume, and bring their own music. The punch cards and tape spools with which this class is dressed symbolize the computer age which had its beginnings in the days when they were in school.

The commencement exercises take place the Monday morning following Alumni Weekend. A great many years ago a commencement ceremony marked the beginning of a student's attempt to earn a degree. Today, of course, it marks the completion of this effort.

At small colleges only a few hundred students may obtain their degrees each year, but at a large university the graduates number in the thousands. At this commencement 3,300 students are to receive degrees. In addition, more than 11,000 mothers, fathers, wives, children, relatives, and friends, all bursting with pride, have come to watch the age-old ceremony.

It begins as seemingly endless files of students in mortarboards and black academic robes move slowly to their seats.

Then hundreds of faculty members and university officials march through the auditorium to their seats on the stage. The leader of the procession carries the university mace, a bronze staff which bears the school's official seal and coat of arms. Atop the mace is an acorn, the symbol of strength and long life.

At almost every commencement a man or a woman who has had a distinguished career in an important field addresses the graduates. At this commencement the speaker was William S. Paley, chairman of the Columbia Broadcasting System and a trustee of the university.

Mr. Paley discussed student demonstrations which that year had erupted on campuses across the country. In most cases, he said, they were justified. He blamed university officials for trying to run the lives of the students without consulting them. He also criticized faculty members for paying too much attention to their own needs and not enough to those of their students. And he urged change.

At small schools graduates usually march to a stage to receive their diplomas from the president. At this university with thousands of graduates this is obviously not practical. Instead the graduates of each school stand together as the president confers their degrees.

"Under the authority vested in me by the university," he declares, "I confer upon you the degree for which you have been recommended, committing you to the rights and privileges which throughout the world pertain to this degree. . . ."

The graduates then tip their mortarboards, as those shown above are doing, the president tips his, and the next group rises. When the exercises are over the diplomas themselves are distributed.

There also are honorary degrees to be awarded. These usually go to men and women outside the university who have made major contributions to society. Here the president and the provost confer an honorary degree on the governor of their state.

The commencement exercises now near their conclusion. The 3,000 graduates stand and sing the university alma mater. The chaplain gives the benediction. The graduates then turn and march from the auditorium in search of a new life.

By early afternoon the university is quiet. In the days that follow, however, many high school students will come here to talk with admissions officers and tour the campus. A number will apply for admission. Of these some will be accepted and the cycle once again will have begun.

The school described in this book is the University of Pennsylvania,
which was founded in 1740 as a small charity school in Philadelphia.
With the help of Benjamin Franklin it grew into one of the nation's
first universities and one of its most distinguished institutions.

164

Publications on Universities and Colleges

Descriptions of Schools and Admissions Procedures

Admissions to College: A Guide for Catholic Students and Their Parents. James W. Arnold, Ralph E. Weber. Milwaukee: Bruce Publishing Co., 1964.

American Junior Colleges. Edmund J. Gleazer, Jr., editor. Washington: American Council on Education. 7th ed. 1967.

American Universities and Colleges. Allan Cartter, editor. Washington: American Council on Education, 1964.

Barron's Profiles of American Colleges. Benjamin Fine. Great Neck, N.Y.: Barron's Educational Series, 1964.

The College Blue Book. Christian E. Burckel, editor. Los Angeles: College Blue Book Co., 1965.

College Entrance Guide. Bernice W. Einstein. New York: Grosset & Dunlap, 1967.

Comparative Guide to American Colleges. James Cass, Max Birnbaum. New York: Harper & Row, 1968.

Complete Planning for College. Sidney Sulkin. New York: McGraw-Hill, 1962.

How to Be Accepted by the College of Your Choice. Benjamin Fine. New York: Channel Press, 1964.

165

Lovejoy's College Guide. Clarence E. Lovejoy. Red Bank, N.J.: Simon & Schuster, 1966.

The New American Guide to College. Gene Hawes. New York: New American Library, 1966.

Financial Assistance

"Borrowing for College." Superintendent of Documents, Government Printing Office (Washington, D.C. 20402), 1965. Free.

"Financial Assistance for College Students: Undergraduate and First Professional." Compiled by Richard C. McKee. Superintendent of Documents, Government Printing Office, 1965. 50¢.

Lovejoy's Scholarship Guide. Clarence E. Lovejoy. Red Bank, N.J.: Simon & Schuster, 1965.

National Register of Scholarships and Fellowships. Juvenal L. Angel. New York: World Trade Academy Press, Inc., 5th ed., 1968.

"Need a Lift?" The American Legion (Dept. S, P.O. Box 1055, Indianapolis, Indiana, 46206), 1966. 25¢.

"Student Assistance Handbook." Superintendent of Documents, Government Printing Office. 60¢.

Acknowledgments

Scores of students, faculty members, and officials at the University of Pennsylvania took time from their responsibilities to talk with me about the university and about their work. A number of outside organizations also were valuable sources of information. In addition, many individuals generously helped with the illustrations in this book. All are listed below or in the Illustration Credits. To each I am deeply grateful.

F. Gerard Adams and his graduate students, Mark W. Allam, Halsey Allen, American Alumni Council, American Association of Colleges, American Association of University Professors, American Association of University Women, George F. Bass, Steven C. Batterman, Mr. and Mrs. Joseph Benner, Rev. Samuel H. Berkowitz, Morton Botel, R. Jean Brownlee, Joseph W. Burk, Lester W. Burket, George Burrell, Clark E. Bussey, William L. Carr, Stuart H. Carroll, Chi Omega, Tristram P. Coffin, College Entrance Examination Board, Community Involvement Council, Joseph Cooper, Robert F. Coryell, Douglas Cownie, Douglas L. Cox, George H. Crumb.

Daily Pennsylvanian, H. C. Deutschlander, Douglas R. Dickson, Leonard C. Dill, Jr., Theodore J. Driesch, Martin Duffy, Educational

Testing Service, Gordon W. Ellis, Alice F. Emerson, Edwin S. Fabricus, Robert M. Figlio, Trisha A. Flynn, Jefferson B. Fordham, John E. Free, Karen Gaines, Louis A. Girifalco, David R. Goddard, Thomas B. A. Godfrey, Marguerite Goff.

Warren J. Haas, Gaylord P. Harnwell, Frederic Harper, Theodore Hershberg, Arleigh P. Hess, Jr., John C. Hetherston, John N. Hobstetter, Evelyn M. Holmes, Gordon Hubel, Michel T. Huber, Theodore H. Husted, Jr., Rev. Stanley E. Johnson, John R. Kershner, Trudy King, Reinout P. Kroon, Thomas F. Lang, Arthur J. Letcher, A. Leo Levin, Harold E. Manley, Alfred K. Mann, Stephen X. Marmon, Nathaniel M. Martin, Mask and Wig, Jeanne McCleary, Walter K. McFarlane, Harrison McMichael, Howard E. Mitchell, Robert B. Mitchell, George A. Munger, Rev. James J. Murphy.

Ted A. Nash, National Center for Educational Statistics, National Education Association, National Interfraternity Council, National Scholarship Service and Fund for Negro Students, Mary Nocella, Robert H. Odell, Priscilla Ord, Robert Osborn, William G. Owen, Arthur R. Owens, Phi Kappa Sigma, Ralph C. Preston, Psi Upsilon, Jonathan Rawle, Alfred J. Reiber, Thomas A. Reiner, John E. Reinhold, Curtis Reitz, Robert M. Rhodes, Gerald L. Robinson, Robert P. Roche, Karen Romer, James F. Ross, Rev. John A. Russell, Jr.

Hidemi Sato, George F. Sawyer, J. Crosier Schaefer, Rev. John M. Scott, Donald T. Sheehan, Larry Simon, Colby Smith and the students in his dormitory section, John P. Smith, Robert E. Smith, Wesley D. Smith, Society for African and Afro-American Students, Alan Soler, Southern Educational Foundation, Tau Epsilon Phi, William H. Telfer, University of Pennsylvania Interfraternity Council, University of Pennsylvania Student Government, University of Pennsylvania Vietnam Week Committee, Roger H. Walmsley, Ned B. Williams, Margaret F. Willson, Mr. and Mrs. David Wilson, Marvin E. Wolfgang, Frank B. Wood, Joan Woolcott, Christine Young and the students in her dormitory section, Alexander V. Zvegintzov.

Illustration Credits

More than half the photographs in this book were taken by Samuel Nocella, Jr. These were supplemented by illustrations provided by the University of Pennsylvania and other sources. When more than one illustration appears on a page, the letter A *next to a page number indicates a top or left position. The letter* B *indicates a bottom or right position.*

The photographs by Mr. Nocella appear on the following pages: 8, 11, 12, 13, 18, 25, 28, 33, 37, 38, 39 A, B, 40, 44, 47, 48, 49, 51 A, B, 52, 54, 62, 63, 65, 66, 67, 68 A, 69, 71, 76, 80, 81, 82, 83, 85, 87, 89, 90, 91, 94, 95, 100, 106 A, B, 107 A, B, 117, 119, 120, 122, 123, 124, 125 B, 126, 127, 128, 129, 131, 138, 144, 145, 146, 150 A, B, 152 A, B, 153, 154, 157, 158, 159, 160, 161, 162 B, 163, 164.

Other illustrations were prepared by the photographers, artists, and university divisions listed below.

Eileen C. Ahrenholz: 10, 72 A, B, 73 A, B, 88; Mike Brodine: 15; Sam Falk *(New York Times):* 136; Harry Gehlert (University Hospital): 93; Robert Hodgson: 113, 114 A, 115; Walter Holt: 50 A, B, 55, 79, 86, 132, 143, 149, 155, 156 A, B, 162 A; Waldemar Illing: 110; Ken Kaplan *(Daily Pennsylvanian):* 139; Michael Katzev: 109; Mary Ellen Mark: 42, 70; Joseph Nettis: 45, 92; Princeton-Pennsylvania Accelerator: 121; James Purring: 43, 98; Donald M. Rosencrantz: 112, 114 B; Frank Ross: 16, 29, 30 A, B, 31 A, B, 32, 34 A, B, 60, 68 B, 74, 75, 84, 96, 97, 140; Hidemi Sato: 108; University Athletic Department: 77; University Economics Department: 133, 134; University Law School, 135; University Physics Department 125 A; Frederick Van Doornick: 111; Bill Vitka *(Daily Pennsylvanian):* 56-57; George S. Zimbel (College Entrance Examination Board): 21.

Index

Business majors, 31

"Campusing," as penalty for curfew violation, 65
Cancer, and research on mitosis, 109
Catacombs (coffeehouse), 82, 138
Center for Studies in Criminology, 116
Chaplains, in university, 137–38
Chicago Symphony Orchestra, Crumb's music played by, 129–30
Christian Association, 82
Chromosomes, research on, 105–108
"Circle music," by Crumb, 129
Civil rights, faculty involved with, 130
Classes, size of, 36
Cold war, 104
Commencement exercises, 157–62
Committee on Student Discipline, 66
Community colleges, 15
Community Involvement Council, 70
Computer tapes, 11
Conscientious objection, chaplains' advice on, 137–38
Costs, of attending university, 26–27, 85–86, 148; see also Expenses
Counselors, guidance, 19, 29, 49
Course Guide, 41
Crew race, 82; trying out for, 30
Criminology, Center for Studies in, 116
Crumb, George, 128–29, 130
Curfew violation, 64; penalty for, 65

Dating, by students, 48

Defense Department, U.S., 17, 59, 105
Delinquents, juvenile, study of, 116–18
Demonstrations, student, 17, 59, 60, 61, 160
Dental school, 94
Dirty Drug (luncheonette), 81, 139
Doctoral dissertation, 91; see also Thesis
Dormitories, for freshmen, 49
Dow Chemical Company, 59, 60, 61
Draft, and chaplains, 137, 138
Drugs, used by students, 47

"Echoes of Time and the River," by Crumb, 128–29
Economic theory, courses in, 35
Economists, at university, 133–34
Electives, minimum of courses in, 35; and "pass-fail" system, 64
Employment specialists, at university, 145
Endowment, university's, 149
Engineering, schools of, 10
English, courses in, 35
Examinations: entrance, 21–23; final, 154; first hourly, 44
Expenses, university's, 147, 148; see also Costs
Extracurricular activities, 24, 30

Faculty, 40–41, 66, 101–39, 141, 143; and administration, 146; involved with social problems, 130–33; junior, 102; number of members of, 102; research by, 103, 104, 105; salaries of, 102, 147; senior, 102; see also Professors
Field hockey, 80

171

172

174

About the author

ALVIN SCHWARTZ is a native of New York City. He is a graduate of Colby College and obtained an M.S. degree in journalism from Northwestern University. After graduation he worked as a newspaper reporter and held jobs in public relations and advertising. For several years he was Director of Communications at the Opinion Research Corporation at Princeton.

Since 1964 he has devoted his time to writing for young people on the social sciences and the arts, and for adults on recreational activities. In addition he teaches English on a part-time basis at Rutgers University.

Mr. Schwartz writes: "My serious books are for young people largely because they are the most important audience I know of." *University* is part of a body of work on American institutions and movements which he is developing for this audience.

Mr. Schwartz and his wife and four children make their home in Princeton, New Jersey.